TO
KILL
AGAIN

TO KILL AGAIN

The Motivation
and Development
of Serial Murder

Donald J. Sears

A Scholarly Resources Imprint
Wilmington, Delaware

©1991 by Scholarly Resources Inc.
All rights reserved
First published 1991
Printed and bound in the United States of America

Scholarly Resources Inc.
104 Greenhill Avenue
Wilmington, DE 19805-1987

Library of Congress Cataloging-in-Publication Data

Sears, Donald J., 1960–
      To kill again : the motivation and development of serial
murder / Donald J. Sears.
            p.   cm.
      Includes bibliographical references and index.
      ISBN 0-8420-2378-X
      1. Serial murders—United States. I. Title.
HV6529.S43   1991
364.1′523′0973—dc20   90-19292
                                                                              CIP

For the victims,
especially those still living

About the Author

Donald J. Sears has degrees in criminology and law and currently practices law in New Jersey. This is his first book.

Contents

Introduction

The act of murder has long been a part of the human experience. Throughout the centuries it has become entrenched in society as an ever-present element of daily life. Traditionally, the reasons for murder were self-evident: a lovers' quarrel becomes heated and results in bloodshed; the discovery of infidelity in a mate leads the spouse to a jealous act of revenge; hungry for riches the armed bandit's greed pushes him toward violence; or, driven by insanity, the deranged psychotic fulfills the commands of an inner evil spirit. Although these reasons have never been condoned, they have been understood. Each of these murderers has had a motive that could be readily identified.

With a devastatingly lethal effect, serial murder has emerged in our culture. It continues to baffle both law enforcement and society because of its inexplicable nature. Accounts of serial murder are appearing with increasing regularity in the headlines, and the news of one man killing twenty, thirty, or even one hundred people shocks the nation each time it occurs. What is most frightening is that these multiple murders seem to be committed for no reason.

Unlike the mass murderer, who kills several people in one violent outburst, the serial murderer takes many lives at random and at will over a period of days, weeks, months, or even years, usually one at a time. In most cases, his victims are complete strangers, both to him and to each other. He may concentrate on one geographic area, or he may travel from state to state, preying on the unsuspecting and the weak and feeling no remorse for his crimes. He is a seemingly cold-blooded, methodical murderer with no definable motive for his behavior. Confronted with such a patternless and irrational method of murder, the police often find themselves frustrated in their attempts to identify and capture this proficient criminal.

Most of society envisions that such an individual is hopelessly insane, or that he appears outwardly evil and therefore is readily detectable. However, this is not the case. In fact, what is perhaps the most frightening characteristic of the serial killer is that he usually presents to the public an image of the all-American boy, the nice man next door, or the shy, quiet neighbor down the street. Often very intelligent, he may appear as a successful, well-respected model citizen in his community; he is the last person anyone would suspect of committing a horrible crime. Yet, underneath this benevolent appearance lies a driven killer who stalks his prey with determined fervor.

The serial murderer has become a nationwide problem of alarming proportions. Some researchers estimate that since 1980 murders with unknown motives have increased by 270 percent.[1] Official crime statistics confirm this, reporting that in 1988 as many as 4,859 murders were committed in the United States by someone with an unclear or unknown reason.[2] In 1983, during U.S. Senate subcommittee hearings held on serial murder, it was found that from 10,000 to 12,000 people per year are murdered by strangers,[3] and that as many as 5,000 of these are the victims of serial killers.[4] Law enforcement officials estimate that there are anywhere from 35 to 500 serial murderers at large in the United States,[5] and it is believed that of all homicides since 1983 one in four has been committed by a serial murderer.[6] Moreover, it is feared that, even with our present knowledge of these individuals, society is still essentially defenseless against these intelligent, dedicated criminals.[7]

This study attempts to unlock the mystery surrounding the phenomena of serial murder and serial murderers. By way of example, Theodore Bundy and John Gacy will be examined in depth to illustrate the life-style of a serial killer. By comparing these two men with other serial murderers, a profile of common characteristics will be formulated. With this profile, various theories of aggressive behavior from the fields of psychology, sociology, and biology are applied to the problem of serial murder. As a result of these findings, we will then be able to establish how the serial murderer develops and what motivates his criminal acts. Once the cause of the problem is identified, efforts can be directed toward the prevention of serial murder. In this way, the senseless slaughter of innocent lives can be stopped.

Notes

1. Egger at 47.
2. *Uniform Crime Reports, 1988* at 13–14.
3. Senate Hearing, July 12, 1983, at 29.
4. Holmes and DeBurger (1988) at 19.
5. Statement of Robert Heck, U.S. Department of Justice, from the film *Murder: No Apparent Motive*. See also Wilson (Paul) at 49; Holmes and DeBurger (1988) at 21; and Norris and Birnes at 19.
6. Cartel at ix.
7. Michaud and Aynesworth at 318.

1 Theodore Robert Bundy

An intelligent, handsome, and well-liked young man in 1974, Theodore Robert Bundy's list of accomplishments was impressive: law student, precinct committeeman of the Republican party, active in the campaign to reelect Washington Governor Dan Evans, and psychiatric counselor for a twenty-four-hour crisis clinic. He was described at various times as the perfect student, a genius, as handsome as a movie idol, a sensitive psychiatric social worker, and "a young man for whom the future could surely hold only success." Even after sentencing Bundy to death for the brutal murders of two college roommates, Judge Edward D. Cowart reflected to Ted: "You're a bright young man. I would have loved to have had you practice law before me. You would have made a good lawyer."[1] For some reason, though, Bundy, this personification of the all-American boy, murdered at least twenty-one young women, from Washington state to Florida, and is believed to have killed many more. Although his deadly spree spanned several years, no one suspected him, and no one knew the terrible truth, until it was much too late.

Ted Bundy was born Theodore Robert Cowell on November 24, 1946. Because his mother was unmarried at the time, she traveled from Philadelphia to give birth at the Elizabeth Lund Home for Unwed Mothers in Burlington, Vermont. She then returned to Philadelphia to live with Ted at her parents' home. Ann Rule, in *The Stranger beside Me*, reports that, while living there, Ted was told that his mother was his sister and his grandparents were his parents. Whether this is true or not is uncertain.[2] What is clear is that he was very close to his grandfather Cowell, who doted upon him. At the age of four, Ted's mother changed his name to Theodore Robert Nelson and moved with him to Tacoma, Washington, in order to protect him from the ridicule of being called a bastard. Leaving his beloved grand-father was a traumatic experience, from which Ted never quite recovered.

One year after arriving in Tacoma, his mother married John Bundy, but, despite his new name, Ted still considered himself a Cowell. His new stepfather was a short, shy man who seemed kind and solid. He was a Boy Scout leader and often took his troop camping, although Ted always had an excuse for not going. In fact, he spent time with his stepfather only grudgingly. The two became increasingly removed from one another, and a loving relationship never developed between them.[3]

When he was a teenager, Ted inadvertently found out that he was illegitimate when a cousin teased him about it. At first he did not believe it was true but later was convinced after being shown his birth certificate. Upset by his cousin's cruelty and furious with his mother for not telling him and leaving him unprepared for this kind of humiliation, Ted remained bitter for a long time.[4] In 1969, when he was twenty-three, he traveled to Vermont and finally saw for himself that his father was unidentified on his birth records.

By junior high school, Ted had developed into a fairly intel-ligent but extremely shy and withdrawn young man, almost introverted. During gym class, for example, he insisted on showering in privacy. Scornful of his shyness the other boys poured water on him, humiliating him and making him angry. In senior high school, Ted was well known but not in the top crowd. He maintained a B average and often studied alone until late at night. In 1965, Ted started college at the University of Puget Sound, and in 1966 he transferred to the University of Washington, where he worked a series of menial jobs, each one usually lasting only a few months. He excelled, however, as a psychology major and became enthralled with the subject. In addition, he found crime stories fascinating, and he read numerous detective magazines, becoming quite knowledgeable on criminal tech-niques.[5] He was even employed for a time as a campus security guard.

Once in college, Ted yearned for a serious relationship but was held back by his shyness and his feeling that he was not socially adept. He believed that his background was stultifyingly middle class and that he had nothing to offer the kind of woman he wanted. He attributed this deficiency in his life to the Bundy family, for whom he felt bitter resentment. A friend related that Ted often stressed how John Bundy was not his real father, was not very bright, and did not make much money. Indeed, he was scornful of what he called the "lack of IQ" of the entire Bundy clan.[6]

Sometime in 1966 or 1967, Ted developed a preoccupation with sex and violence and sought out pornographic materials that centered on the use, abuse, and possession of women as objects.[7] Later he stated that this may have been a way of vicariously experiencing that which in reality he could not. Although this fantasized possession of women soon gave way to a more active form of gratification, he kept this aspect of his life completely hidden, thereby continuing his appearance as the all-American boy.

Ted had his first sexual encounter at age twenty, when he met Stephanie Brooks[8] at the University of Washington. He was deeply infatuated with this strikingly beautiful woman with long dark hair parted down the middle. She was from a wealthy family, and Ted therefore believed that he had little to offer her. They were together only one year when it became apparent that he was more in love with her than she was with him. Indeed, Stephanie had become disillusioned; he was foundering in college and had no real plans or prospects for the future. Emotional and unsure of himself, Ted began using people by becoming close to those who might do him favors and then taking advantage of their friendship.

Stephanie finally told Ted that their relationship was over and that their lives were headed on divergent paths. She was the personification of everything he wanted and now she was leaving him; he was devastated by her rejection. Ted convinced himself that she was too beautiful and too rich for him.[9] Although he returned to her in the hopes of rekindling their romance, he was spurned again. As a result, he resolved to change and become the kind of man that the world—and particularly Stephanie—would see as a success.

From all outward appearances, Ted indeed changed almost immediately. He became active in the Republican party, particularly in the campaign to reelect Governor Dan Evans, and eventually he held the position of precinct committeeman. In

1970 he was commended by the Seattle Police Department for running down a purse snatcher and returning the stolen bag to its owner. In addition, he rushed into Green Lake in Seattle's North End and saved a three-and-one-half-year-old toddler from drowning.[10] He also became a successful rape crisis counselor at the Seattle Crisis Clinic.

Shortly after his relationship with Stephanie had ended, Ted became involved with Meg Anders,[11] who was a sharp contrast to Stephanie. Meg was small, vulnerable, and shy, and she clung to Ted at parties. Although he claimed that he loved her, he confessed that he could not stop thinking about Stephanie. Ann Rule, with whom he worked at the Seattle Crisis Clinic, explains that, although Stephanie had ended their relationship in 1968, Ted spoke in 1972 as if the intervening years had not happened at all. He apparently struggled with the dilemma of staying with Meg or seeking out Stephanie.[12]

Eventually, while still involved with Meg, Ted returned to Stephanie, who liked the new Ted. Apparently he had become a mature, successful, handsome young man who was charming and articulate. He professed his love for her through expensive gifts and luxurious dinners and treated her with tenderness and affection; she reciprocated in kind. All this was kept a complete secret from Meg, with whom Ted continued to maintain a serious relationship. In September 1973, Ted informed Stephanie that the two of them were engaged, and Stephanie was elated. In December, however, he quite unexpectedly ended their relationship. His whole attitude toward her had somehow changed, and he was uninterested in and even hostile toward Stephanie, who was shocked and hurt.

It later became apparent that between 1967 and 1973 Ted had been lying extensively, not only to Meg but also to college professors and friends. He thus manipulated his way through difficult times with Meg, convinced friends of his importance, and persuaded others to loan him money. Furthermore, accomplishments he bragged about and put on his résumé were only ideas that he never carried out. For example, a study on rape that he boasted of writing, as well as a story on the racial significance in jury composition, was never even begun.[13] Although he had no adult criminal record while in college, it is known that he often stole items from stores, including televisions, textbooks, and ski boots, and was pleased that he was able to do so without getting caught. As a juvenile, however, Ted had had several brushes with the law. It is reported that he was picked up at least twice for suspicion of auto theft and burglary, but any records have long since been destroyed.[14]

In 1973, Ted applied to several law schools but was rejected by all but the University of Utah College of Law. This was a major setback for his ego, as he had expected a flood of acceptances. When it came time to start the fall semester at Utah, Ted wrote the dean of admissions that he would not be attending, explaining that he was recovering from injuries sustained in a serious auto accident. In reality, he had no such injuries.

Although Ted continued to project an outward facade of the all-American boy with a successful future, there was another side that would become horribly frightening. In *The Only Living Witness*, Stephen G. Michaud and Hugh Aynesworth relate how Bundy began to prowl the night as a voyeur. By chance one evening he observed a woman undressing through an open window. From that point on he increasingly roamed the community, peering into windows. Indeed, "he approached it almost like a project, throwing himself into it, literally, for years."[15] However, participating only as a spectator eventually failed to satisfy whatever need in Ted it originally had fulfilled, and he soon turned to physical contact. He explained that the first woman he ever hit with a club fell to the ground and screamed. Terrified at the thought of being caught, he panicked and ran. Although Ted described his fear and anxiety about being discovered, there was no mention of remorse toward the victim or what she had suffered.[16]

Bundy's ability to attract and then assault women soon improved until it was honed to a precise science. Although he may have assaulted or killed many others, the first murder attributed to Bundy is that of Katherine Merry Devine,[17] a tall, willowy fifteen-year-old who had disappeared on November 25, 1973. She was last seen hitchhiking and being picked up by a man driving a truck. Shortly thereafter, on December 6, she was found in McKenney Park near Olympia, Washington, her jeans slit up the back seam from the crotch to the waist. She had been sodomized, strangled, and her throat may have been cut, although the body's decomposition made verification of the wound impossible to determine. Ominously, these last months of 1973 had marked Bundy's drastic change in attitude toward Stephanie.

Joni Lentz,[18] a shy, friendly, eighteen-year-old student at the University of Washington, was attacked on January 4, 1974, while she slept in her basement apartment. She was beaten about the head with a metal rod that had been pulled from the bed frame. The rod was then jammed into her vagina causing serious internal damage. She survived after remaining in a coma for several months.

On February 1, 1974, Lynda Ann Healy, a tall, slender, twenty-one-year-old University of Washington student with long chestnut hair and blue eyes, also was killed while asleep in her basement apartment less than one mile from where Joni Lentz had been murdered. She had been beaten about the head and then carried off. The next morning her roommates found her bed neatly made, but when they pulled the covers back found the sheets covered with dried blood. They also discovered her bloodied nightgown hanging neatly in the closet. Lynda's attacker had apparently taken the time to make the bed and dress her before carrying her away. Her skull, obviously crushed by a blunt instrument, was found on March 12, 1975, on Washington's Taylor Mountain.

On March 12, 1974, Donna Gail Manson, age nineteen, five feet tall, 100 pounds, with blue eyes and long brown hair, disappeared while on her way to a jazz concert near Olympia. Friends related how she was obsessed with death and magic and often would embark upon hitchhiking excursions without warning. Six days after her disappearance, the police filed a standard missing persons report and assumed that she was a runaway.[19] She has never been found.

On April 17, 1974, Susan Elaine Rancourt disappeared. She was a shy, quiet, intelligent, eighteen-year-old who was five feet two inches tall, 120 pounds, and had blue eyes and long blonde hair. In accordance with police departmental policy,[20] her disappearance was treated for the first forty-eight hours as if she had run away. Only her skull, which had been fractured, was recovered on March 7, 1975, on Taylor Mountain eighty-seven miles from where she last had been seen.

Roberta Kathleen Parks disappeared from Oregon State University shortly before 11:00 P.M. on May 6, 1974. At age twenty-two she was tall and slender and had long ash-blonde hair. On March 10, 1975, her skull, which had been crushed by a blunt instrument, was the only part of her body found, on Taylor Mountain 262 miles from where she had disappeared.

Brenda Carol Ball, a twenty-two-year-old, standing five feet three inches and weighing 112 pounds, disappeared about 2:00 A.M. on June 1, 1974, from the Flame Tavern in Burien, Washington. The only part of her body recovered was her skull, which was found on March 1, 1975, thirty miles away, also on Taylor Mountain; it had been crushed on the left side by a blunt instrument.

On June 11, 1974, Georgeann Hawkins, eighteen, five feet two inches tall, and 115 pounds, disappeared from the University of Washington campus. An honor student with brown eyes and long brown hair, she was last seen around 1:00 A.M. as she walked toward her sorority house. Initially, the Seattle police took no action at all. After news of her disappearance was broadcast on local television the next day, an investigation was begun.[21] She has never been found.

On July 17, 1974, Janice Anne Ott, age twenty-three, and Denise Naslund, age eighteen, both disappeared from Washington's Lake Sammamish State Park. Janice, who was five feet and weighed 100 pounds, had long brown hair parted down the middle. She was last seen around 12:30 P.M. accompanying a good-looking man with an English accent who called himself "Ted." His arm was in a sling, and he asked for help with his sailboat, which did not exist. Denise was five feet four inches, weighed 120 pounds, had long dark hair, and was last seen around 4:30 P.M. with a man with an English accent calling himself "Ted." His arm was in a sling.

Police response to these disappearances was swift, and hundreds of witnesses were questioned, from which a composite sketch of "Ted" was made. Anyone with this name was considered a potential suspect. Aerial infrared photographs were taken of the state park with no results. In addition, a local psychiatrist developed a profile of the assailant: "Ted" was between twenty-five and thirty-five years old, mentally ill, and was a man who feared women and their power over him.[22] Despite these efforts, no substantial leads were developed. Both women were found in

September 1974 four miles from the park, close to Taylor Mountain. They had been strangled or bludgeoned to death.

Carol Valenzuela,[23] age twenty, disappeared on August 2, 1974, from Vancouver. Her body, along with the remains of an unidentified female in her late teens or early twenties, was found in October 1974, some miles south of Olympia. Carol had been strangled.

After the disappearance of Carol Valenzuela, however, the abductions in the northwest seemed to end. Washington state investigators theorized that the suspect was in jail for another crime, had left the area, or was dead.[24] They did not know that to the south, in Utah, the murders continued. Ted Bundy had moved from Washington state to start the 1974 fall semester at the University of Utah College of Law. At first he maintained a C average but soon began drinking much more than in the past; consequently, his grades continued to drop. Nevertheless, to those around him he appeared to be a bright, articulate, blossoming young attorney.

In October the abductions resumed. Nancy Wilcox,[25] age sixteen, disappeared from Holladay, Utah, on October 2, 1974. She has never been found. And, on October 18, 1974, Melissa Smith, age seventeen, five feet three inches, 105 pounds, with long, light brown hair parted down the middle, disappeared shortly after 10:00 P.M. from Midvale, Utah. She was found on the 27th near Summit Park, Utah, in the Wasatch Mountains. She had been beaten savagely about the head, possibly with a crowbar, and had been strangled with her own stockings, raped, and sodomized.

Laura Aime, who was seventeen, six feet, 115 pounds, with long hair, disappeared from Lehi, Utah, on October 31, 1974, shortly after midnight. She was found on Thanksgiving Day in the Wasatch Mountains. Her head had been battered so severely that her face was unrecognizable; it was thought that an iron crowbar had been used. She was also strangled with her own stockings and sexually assaulted.

On November 8, 1974, Carol DaRonch, age eighteen, was approached in the Fashion Place Mall in Murray, Utah, by a man identifying himself as Officer Roseland. He told her that a robbery had just taken place and asked her to step outside, where he then coaxed her into his Volkswagen and started to drive away.

Suddenly, he clamped handcuffs on one of her wrists and attempted to cuff the other when she managed to pull away. He then tried to hit her with a crowbar but was thwarted when she escaped and ran into the street and hailed a passing motorist. This incident occurred less than one mile from where Melissa Smith had disappeared.

On that same night, November 8, 1974, Debra Kent, age seventeen, with long brown hair parted down the middle, disappeared from a high school play in Bountiful, Utah, seventeen miles from where Carol DaRonch had been attacked. The Utah police did not respond immediately but waited until the following morning to begin a search of the high school.[26] She has never been found.

By this time, Meg Anders began to suspect that Ted Bundy was somehow involved in these disappearances. When the abductions began in Utah, she noticed the similarities between the Utah killings and those that had occurred in Washington. She contacted the Salt Lake City police and informed them that Bundy, who fit the description of the Washington "Ted," recently moved to Utah.[27] However, there was clearly not enough evidence to justify an arrest. He could not be placed at the scene of any of the murders, and much of what Meg and the police believed was mere speculation. Then, suddenly, the Utah abductions ended. Bundy was now concentrating his efforts in Colorado.

On January 12, 1975, Caryn Campbell, twenty-three years old, five feet four inches, with long brown shoulder-length hair, disappeared from the Wildwood Inn in Aspen, Colorado, around 9:45 P.M. Police responded to her disappearance as a routine missing persons case; they did not begin to search for her until the following morning.[28] She was found on February 18, 1975, just a few miles from the inn. Although her body had deep cuts made from a sharp weapon, she died from repeated blows to the head by a blunt instrument. Very little skin tissue was left on the neck, but it appeared that she had been strangled as well.

On March 15, 1975, Julie Cunningham, age twenty-six, with dark hair parted down the middle, disappeared from a Vail, Colorado, ski resort around 9:00 P.M. She has never been found.

On April 6, 1975, Denise Oliverson, twenty-five years old, with long dark hair, disappeared while riding her bicycle in Grand Junction, Colorado. Treating the case as a routine disappearance and not as a homicide, the police conducted a superficial search. They found her bicycle and shoes underneath a bridge not far from where she was last seen. Shortly thereafter the bicycle was stolen from the police department's bicycle rack, and therefore it was never examined for fingerprints.[29] She has never been found.

Melanie Cooley,[30] age eighteen, who looked enough like Debra Kent to be her twin, disappeared on April 15, 1975. Last seen in Nederland, Colorado, fifty miles west of Denver, she was found on April 23, 1975, twenty miles from where she had disappeared. She had been bludgeoned about the head with a rock, her hands were tied, and a pillowcase was twisted tightly around her neck.

Shelly K. Robertson,[31] age twenty-four, disappeared on July 1, 1975, from Golden, Colorado. A frequent hitchhiker, she was last seen in the company of a wild-haired man driving a pickup truck. She was found on August 21, 1975, 500 feet inside a mine shaft not far from Vail. And, on that same day, Nancy Baird,[32] age twenty-one, disappeared from a service station in Farmington, Utah. She has never been found.

As the killings continued in this manner they seemed to occur more and more frequently with the passing weeks. Police found themselves frustrated because the crime scenes rendered no clues as to the identity of the assailant. Eventually, Bundy was arrested, although not for murder or assault but for possession of burglary tools. While cruising through a quiet neighborhood around 3:00 A.M. on August 16, 1975, he parked on the side of a darkened street. From behind, an unmarked police patrol car flashed its high beams at Bundy. Suddenly, his Volkswagen lurched forward and sped away without its headlights on. The officer attempted to pull Bundy over, but he only drove faster. With his headlights now on, Bundy ran through two stop signs and swerved around a turn. Then, suddenly, he pulled into a vacant gas station lot and stopped. Upon questioning, he was caught several times in a lie about what he was doing, when he said that he had been to see a particular movie that was not showing at the theater. In his car, the police discovered a crowbar, ski mask, rope, wire, plastic garbage bags, a flashlight, ice picks, a panty hose mask, and a set of handcuffs.[33] He seemed amused that the police considered any of these items as burglars' tools and casually attempted to explain everything.

After Bundy was taken into custody for the possession of burglary tools, a detective glanced at the arrest report and recalled that Meg Anders had identified a Ted Bundy as a possible suspect in the slayings. He reviewed the DaRonch and Kent files and noticed that Bundy fit the description of the assailant given by witnesses in those cases. After looking at several photographs, Carol DaRonch positively identified Bundy, as did a teacher who saw him at Bountiful High School the night Debbie Kent disappeared.[34] In addition, police examined Bundy's gas credit card charges, trying to determine his whereabouts at the time of each victim's disappearance. What they discovered was startling. Bundy had put a tremendous amount of miles on his car, sometimes 420 in one day. For example, on January 12, the day Caryn Campbell disappeared, he had purchased gas in Glenwood, Colorado. The next day he bought gas in Green River, Utah, and then in Salt Lake City.

From the credit card slips, a clear pattern of driving habits emerged, starting with a lull but then increasing over a period of approximately thirty days. At the peak of this activity, Bundy was in the same area where a victim was abducted. Afterward, the lull in driving returned but only for one or two weeks. It then became a frightening pattern of what one investigator coined Ted's "trolling," or fishing for a victim.[35]

On March 1, 1976, Bundy was found guilty of aggravated kidnapping in the Carol DaRonch case and sentenced to one to fifteen years in the Utah State Prison. On January 27, 1977, he was taken from the prison and extradited to Aspen, Colorado, to stand trial for the murder of Caryn Campbell. The Colorado authorities had been amassing evidence against him since his arrest in Utah. When interrogated, Bundy denied ever being in Colorado, much less the Wildwood Inn. However, in his apartment police found a map of Colorado that had come from the inn. In addition, hair samples taken from Bundy's Volkswagen were identified as those of Campbell, as well as Melissa Smith and Carol DaRonch. The crowbar found in his car matched the tear in Campbell's head, and a woman from the Wildwood Inn identified Bundy as the man she had seen in the hotel on the night of Campbell's disappearance.[36] Although he left more victims in

Washington state and Utah, it was in Colorado that his chance of conviction was greatest.

In Aspen, Bundy made his first attempt to escape by jumping from an open second-story courthouse window and fleeing to the Colorado hills. After eluding the police for 133 hours, he was finally recaptured. He did not remain in prison long. On December 30, 1977, he escaped from the Garfield County jail, this time for good. Upon reaching freedom, Bundy made his way to Florida, arriving in Tallahassee on January 8, 1978. He assumed the name Chris Hagen and rented an apartment near the Florida State University campus, vowing that he would do nothing to cause law enforcement officers to even glance his way.[37] This promise was tragically short-lived.

On January 15, 1978, only one week after Bundy had arrived in Florida, four young women, students at Florida State, were savagely attacked as they slept in the Chi Omega Sorority House. Some time between 2:45 and 3:00 A.M., Bundy crept into the house and attacked the girls, beginning with twenty-one-year-old Margaret Bowman, who was bludgeoned on the head with such fierceness that her skull was shattered, with bits of bone lodging in her brain. She was then strangled with a nylon stocking that Bundy had brought with him. She was not sexually assaulted, but he left rope burns on her left thigh when he viciously pulled off her panties.

Next was Lisa Levy, age twenty, who died from strangulation. She was beaten about the head and collarbone, and the nipple of her right breast was bitten almost completely off. She also received a double bite to her left buttock, where Bundy had bitten her twice. She was sexually assaulted but probably after being attacked with a Clairol hair mist bottle (both rectally and vaginally). The other two victims, Kathy Kleiner and Karen Chandler, both twenty-one, were roommates. Each was clubbed about the head and face, apparently with a tree branch taken from a pile of logs outside the sorority house, and received skull fractures, broken teeth, and a broken jaw. For some unknown reason, Bundy left at that point, and Kathy and Karen survived.

This was not the end of Bundy's vicious frenzy, however. On that same night, eight blocks away, Cheryl Thomas, age twenty-one, was bludgeoned about the head and received skull fractures, a broken jaw, and permanent hearing loss in one ear. She was attacked around 4:00 A.M. while she slept, and her bed clothes were torn from her body. She, too, survived.

The killings then subsided for a short time, but on February 8, 1978, Bundy was again on the prowl. Driving a stolen van, he pulled up next to Leslie Ann Parmenter,[38] age fourteen, in Jacksonville, Florida, two hundred miles east of Tallahassee. Wearing a false moustache and calling himself Richard Burton, Bundy showed the girl a false fireman's badge and asked her to get in the van. Contrary to his normally confident and convincing manner, he was nervous, agitated, and trembling. He was unshaven, his clothes were disheveled, his speech was awkward, and he had a strange look that frightened Leslie.[39] Before Bundy could coax her into the van her older brother arrived, and Bundy hurriedly retreated. The next young girl would not be so lucky.

The following day, February 9, 1978, Kimberly Diane Leach, a pretty twelve-year-old with long brown hair, was picked up from her schoolyard by a man in a white van. Bundy was seen "scolding" Kimberly and leading her to the van; he recklessly drove away with her. On April 7, 1978, she was found in a small shack, naked except for her tennis shoes and white turtleneck shirt. Next to her body were her clothes, placed there neatly by her killer. The cause of death was determined to be penetration of the neck by some unknown object.[40] Because advanced stages of decomposition had set in, authorities were unable to determine if she had been sexually assaulted.

Bundy's killing spree finally ended when he was arrested in Pensacola, Florida, two hundred miles west of Tallahassee, on February 15, 1978, where he was caught driving a stolen car. He had attracted police attention to himself while prowling a quiet neighborhood late at night. Just as in Utah, he first attempted to flee from the officer but then suddenly stopped. When questioned, he tried to strike the officer and flee. He was captured after a short struggle and taken into custody. Interestingly, while en route to police headquarters, Bundy exclaimed: "I wish you'd killed me back there," and later asked: "If I run from you at the jail, then will you kill me?"[41] Even though he was on the FBI's Ten Most Wanted List, police did not realize whom they had just captured until Bundy himself told them. Three days after he was arrested, he telephoned Meg Anders from Florida and related to her that

> there is something the matter with me. It wasn't you. It was me.
> I just couldn't contain it. I've fought it for a long, long time . . .
> it got too strong. We just happened to be going together when
> it got under way. I tried to suppress it. It was taking more and
> more of my time. That's why I didn't do well in school. My time
> was being used trying to make my life look normal. But it
> wasn't normal. All the time I could feel that force building in
> me.[42]

He further stated that fantasies had controlled his life for some
time, claiming that he had fought the urge to kill but that this
force from within simply had consumed him.[43]

Upon comparison, all of Bundy's victims bore striking similarities. They were young Caucasian females, most between the
ages of seventeen and nineteen. All had long hair parted down
the middle, and all were slim, attractive, and highly talented in
some respect. Each was single and had more than average
intelligence. They were shy, quiet girls who gladly would help
someone in need. A majority was attacked at night, and all were
left unburied, wearing little or no clothes. Most were first struck
on the head with some type of blunt instrument and then further
attacked, either by strangulation, stabbing or cutting, or sexual
assault. Very few were raped, although several were sexually
assaulted with various instruments (for example, a steel rod or a
Clairol bottle). Many were college students, although none of the
victims, so far as can be determined, knew Bundy personally.
Many were disposed of in a park or wooded area, and no physical
evidence of the killer was found at any of the murder scenes.

Ann Rule observed that with most of the victims something
in their lives had gone wrong on the day they vanished. Except
for those who were attacked as they slept, all were somehow
preoccupied with depression, illness, worry, or anxiety. Rule
surmises that somehow Bundy knew that his victims were preoccupied, thereby making them vulnerable to attack.[44]

Fortunately, some of Bundy's attempts were frustrated, either
by the appearance of a third person, or by the hesitancy of his
intended victim to accompany him. The accounts these women
give show the pattern of behavior Bundy usually followed in his
attacks. In making his initial contact with a potential victim, he
sometimes wore his arm in a sling or his leg in a cast. In this
seemingly helpless condition, he sought out young women to

assist him, for example, with carrying his books or his briefcase or helping him with a sailboat. At other times he identified himself as a police officer or fireman and displayed a badge. Using his intelligence, physical attractiveness, and articulate speech, he was quickly able to convince a woman of his sincerity and persuade her to get into his car, where her fate was sealed.

Special Agent Robert K. Ressler of the FBI's Behavioral Sciences Unit observes that at first Bundy did not kill until he had lured his victim into his "comfort zone,"[45] which was the front passenger seat of his car. Once there, he incapacitated her, usually by striking the woman sharply in the head with a blunt instrument, rendering her unconscious. Those victims who were not killed in the comfort zone were murdered in their own beds while they slept. Thus, they were unconscious as well when Bundy struck, rendering them just as defenseless as those who were taken in by his "charms." Except for the Chi Omega killings, Bundy removed his victims from the scene of the crime, transporting them in his car to some wilderness area where they were left, not buried but nevertheless concealed.

As the killings progressed, it was obvious that Bundy became more daring and less afraid of getting caught. As noted by investigators, he seemed to be playing a game of challenge, each time taking more chances, seemingly trying to prove that he could continue his criminal acts and not be captured. This may be very true since it was always Ted's opinion that he was above the law and too cunning to be caught. At times, he felt almost immune from detection. While in Florida, he boasted that he knew the law well and was much smarter than any policeman. Likewise, while in Utah awaiting trial, he made a game of the police surveillance efforts. He considered the officers tailing him to be clumsy and awkward and bragged about losing them. He even approached the surveillance teams and chatted with them, taunting them all the while. Even more frightening was that the attacks appeared to be coming closer and closer together. It was as if the awful fixation of the killer needed more frequent stimuli to give him relief.[46]

During the investigation of the murders, several theories evolved as to Bundy's motivations. One psychiatrist predicted that Ted feared women and their power over him, and that he also would exhibit at times socially isolative behavior. Another theory hypothesized that some men are influenced by a pseudomenstrual cycle, whereby they are driven to rape and kill. Still others believed that Bundy suffered from a compulsion to hunt down and murder the same type of woman over and over again and that he could never murder her enough times to find relief.[47]

Ann Rule adopts this last theory and surmises that the victims were all prototypes of Stephanie Brooks, the first woman to reveal Ted's vulnerability and damage his ego. They all resembled her, with the same long hair parted down the middle and the same smooth, symmetrical facial features. Rule posits that Bundy had to kill Stephanie repeatedly, hoping that each time would bring him relief but finding that the more women he murdered the worse his obsession became. Others simply believed that Bundy was a sexual psychopath.[48]

When he was finally caught, psychiatrists labeled Ted a sociopath, a person displaying characteristics of an antisocial personality. He exhibited a lack of guilt feelings; he was callous and had a pronounced tendency to compartmentalize and methodically rationalize his behavior. He was intelligent (IQ 124), and he knew how to manipulate people skillfully. He was confident that he could overcome all adversity, and, when he did not, he blamed his disappointments on others. He was prone to sudden mood swings, which developed into cyclical periods of depression. He also had a strong fascination for violent pornography, bondage, and sodomy. Meg Anders relates how on one occasion he had tied her to the bedposts with nylon stockings and, during intercourse, began choking her.[49]

A complete physical examination of Bundy revealed no clues to his behavior. A brain scan and X rays of his skull showed nothing out of the ordinary. Electroencephalographic readings were unremarkable, and physicians concluded that there was no evidence of organic brain disease or any form of mental impairment. However, one behavioral characteristic that became obvious to both investigators and researchers was how meticulously neat Bundy kept his home. It was apparent that he loved his possessions more than the people with whom he interacted. In fact, he was obsessed with material things and is believed to have kept much of the clothing of the girls he killed.[50]

Once in prison, Bundy enjoyed the publicity he had attracted and considered himself a celebrity. During his incarceration in the Utah and Colorado prisons, he was in constant contact with the news media, either by phone, correspondence, or press conference. Many of his comments were controversial and prejudicial to his case. Even after a circuit court judge in Florida denied Bundy's request for access to the media, he still corresponded with reporters from all over the country, relishing the limelight. During his trials, he continually sought to control the proceedings, commanding the attention of both judge and jury. In Florida, he insisted upon representing himself before the jury on several occasions. Rather than advance his defense, however, he succeeded in emphasizing the gruesome crime scenes and the horror of his acts.[51]

Throughout the court proceedings, Bundy was indifferent to the outcome. His participation was purely for his own amusement. He was never concerned with the severity of the charges against him and displayed no emotion even when sentenced to die. He expressed no remorse for what he had done, believing that guilt was simply an unhealthy mechanism used by society to control people. Indeed, he stated that he "felt sorry for people who feel guilt."[52]

Although Bundy had been scheduled to die in the electric chair on numerous occasions, a last-minute appeal to the state or federal courts always stayed the execution. Finally, the courts simply rejected his appeals, and, after sitting on death row at the Florida State Prison for almost eleven years, Ted Bundy was executed on January 24, 1989. In one last attempt to manipulate those around him, he spent his remaining few days confessing to numerous murders. His apparent strategy was to interest investigators in hearing more details about his killings and thereby invoke their assistance in seeking one more stay of execution.[53] Bundy's plan was unsuccessful.

By talking with investigators from several states before he died, Bundy helped to close thirteen murder cases in Utah, Colorado, and Washington state. He also provided information on fourteen others in Washington, Utah, Idaho, Colorado, Vermont, and Pennsylvania as well as at least twenty more slayings in various states dating from 1969, many with which he had never been associated. In total, his confessions brought the number of murders connected to him to at least fifty, with many believing the toll to be even higher.[54]

Several of those who spoke to Bundy during his last hours described him as tearful, stuttering, remorseful, and seemingly eager to clear his conscience. Indeed, investigators found that the information he provided was accurate, and that his confessions were genuine. Others, however, believed that Bundy's only remorse was that he was finally going to die. Whether he truly felt compassion for his victims will remain a complete unknown. He was pronounced dead at 7:16 A.M.[55]

Notes

1. Rule at 13; *Murder: No Apparent Motive.*
2. Rule at 22. See also Michaud and Aynesworth, who maintain that Bundy always knew that she was his mother and that he called her Mom.
3. Rule at 23.
4. Kendall at 27.
5. Rule at 23; Michaud and Aynesworth at 117.
6. Rule at 48–49.
7. Michaud and Aynesworth at 117–18.
8. This person is identified as Stephanie Brooks in Rule, as Marjorie Russel in Michaud and Aynesworth, as Diane in Larsen, and as Susan Phillips in Kendall. The name Stephanie Brooks will be used in this book.
9. Rule at 27.
10. Id. at 31.
11. This person is identified as Meg Anders in Rule, as Elizabeth Kendall in Kendall and in Michaud and Aynesworth, and as Cas Richter in Larsen. The name Meg Anders will be used in this book.
12. Rule at 38–39.
13. Id. at 44.
14. Kendall at 35; Rule at 24.
15. Much of the material in Michaud and Aynesworth comes from hours of personal interviews that the authors had with Bundy in the Florida State Prison. Bundy's ability to fabricate was one of his most accomplished traits. As such, the accounts he relates must be read with that in mind. For quote see Michaud and Aynesworth at 118.
16. Id. at 121.
17. This person appears in Rule but does not appear in Michaud and Aynesworth or in Larsen.
18. This person is identified as Joni Lentz in Rule, as Sharon Clarke in Larsen, and as Mary Adams in Michaud and Aynesworth. The name Joni Lentz will be used in this book.
19. Egger at 151.
20. Id. at 151–52.
21. Id. at 152.

22. Rule at 94; Egger at 154–55.
23. This person appears in Michaud and Aynesworth and in Larsen but does not appear in Rule.
24. Rule at 98.
25. This person appears in Michaud and Aynesworth and in Larsen but not in Rule.
26. Egger at 152.
27. Cartel at 184.
28. Egger at 153.
29. Id.
30. This person appears in Larsen and Rule but not in Michaud and Aynesworth.
31. This person appears in Larsen and Rule but not in Michaud and Aynesworth.
32. This person appears in Michaud and Aynesworth but not in Rule or Larsen.
33. Larsen at 68–70.
34. Cartel at 185.
35. Larsen at 141.
36. Cartel at 185–87.
37. Michaud and Aynesworth at 194–207; Rule at 17–18, 20.
38. This person appears in Larsen and Rule but not in Michaud and Aynesworth.
39. Rule at 250.
40. Id. at 281.
41. Larsen at 225; Rule at 261.
42. Kendall at 174–75. See also Egger at 140–41.
43. Winn and Merrill at 314; Egger at 145; Kendall at 174.
44. Rule at 118.
45. From an interview conducted for the film *Murder: No Apparent Motive.*
46. Rule at 65, 244, 153, 84.
47. Id. at 86, 84, 115.
48. Id. at 340–41, 84.
49. Michaud and Aynesworth at 319–20; Rule at 188, 136.
50. Leyton at 84; Rule at 135.
51. Egger at 127–28; Larsen at 272; Michaud and Aynesworth at 279–80.
52. Michaud and Aynesworth at 313.
53. "A Diabolical Genius" at 11; Axthelm and Ryan at 46; " 'Deliberate Stranger' Killer Helping Lawmen" at 41.
54. "Bundy Toll May be 50" at A21; Bright at 1.
55. "A Diabolical Genius" at 11; Axthelm and Ryan at 46; Nordheimer at A1.

2 John Wayne Gacy

In 1978, John Gacy was one of the most respected and well-liked members of the Norridge, Illinois, community, a suburb of Chicago. Describing him as gregarious, energetic, polite, and easygoing, friends and neighbors thought highly of him. Professionally, he had established a successful contracting company. He was a precinct captain for the Democratic party, an active member of the local Jaycees, the lighting commissioner of Norridge, and was responsible for putting on several parades throughout Chicago. In addition, he had a reputation for dressing as a circus clown and entertaining children in hospitals and orphanages. A fellow Jaycee member and former Iowa state representative was thoroughly confident that Gacy could have been successful at almost anything.[1] Unknown to the world, however, was Gacy's darker side. While appearing as a pillar of the community, he was secretly murdering young men and boys in and around the Chicago area. When he was finally stopped by police, thirty-three young men were dead,[2] most buried in the crawl space under the floorboards of his home. This thirty-six-year-old success story had been a methodic killing machine for many years.

John Wayne Gacy was born on March 17, 1942, at Edgewater Hospital on Chicago's far North Side.[3] He was the only son of John Gacy, Sr., and Marion Elaine Robinson. He had one sister two years older and another sister two years younger. He attended Catholic school until the age of eleven, when the family moved and he was enrolled in public school.[4] Although an intelligent child, by the end of grade school he was daydreaming in class and had started to resist his teachers.

A source of distraction for young Gacy was his seemingly constant health problems. Born with an enlarged bottleneck

21

heart, he therefore could not participate in any strenuous activities.[5] At age ten he began to experience fainting spells for no reason, but, although he was hospitalized on numerous occasions, the cause of his fainting was never positively determined. Doctors believed, however, that he suffered from recurrent syncope, a brief loss of consciousness caused by transient anemia, leading to probable psychomotor epilepsy.[6] Later in his youth he experienced several epileptic-type seizures, during which he fought and kicked those around him.[7] When he was sixteen years old, his behavior was finally attributed to a blood clot on the brain, which it was thought had resulted from a playground accident. He was treated at that time and reportedly cured.[8] Nevertheless, his blackouts continued into adulthood.

As a young child, Gacy was loving and eager to please but rarely with his father, whose meticulous standards of craftsmanship he was unable to meet, and, when he failed, his father called him stupid. The older Gacy was hard working, a perfectionist, a stern parent, and a good provider, but he was also a drunkard and a wife beater. One evening when Gacy's mother was recently home from the hospital with her third child, his father began to beat her, knocking out several teeth. He chased her out of the house onto the street and continued to pummel her until the police arrived. As John, Jr., grew he tried to intercede in these scenes but was always belittled by his father, who called him a mama's boy or a sissy.[9]

Gacy finished his elementary education at a vocational school, where his conduct received generally favorable ratings.[10] Although he attended four different high schools, he never completed his senior year. As a teenager, he developed what one of his brothers-in-law later described as a "hang-up" with uniforms. He had always dreamed of becoming a policeman but could not because of his physical ailments.[11] Thus, while still in high school, Gacy became active in the civil defense, which allowed him to display a blue light on his car. Whenever there was a fire or accident, he sped off to the scene, flashing his light.[12]

After dropping out of high school, Gacy left Chicago for Las Vegas, where he found part-time employment at the Palm Mortuary. The manager recalled Gacy as a polite, cooperative young man and doubts that he had much contact with the bodies since his duties were mostly janitorial.[13] One author, however, reports that Gacy, noticing that a dead boy at the mortuary had developed an erection at death, crawled into the casket with the body. Gacy moved back to Chicago the day after this incident supposedly took place, apparently frightened by the experience.[14]

After returning to Chicago, Gacy began work as a shoe salesman and was an instant success. His articulate and ingratiating manner, together with his loquacious nature, suited him to the profession. He also began dating frequently, and, after a nine-month courtship, he married a local woman. Soon thereafter the couple had their first child, a son, and Gacy seemed to be a devoted and loving husband and father. However, it was right after his wife's pregnancy that he had his first homosexual experience, explaining that while drunk a friend had performed fellatio on him.[15] It would not be his last encounter.

Gacy moved his young family to Waterloo, Iowa, when his father-in-law offered him a manager's position at a Kentucky Fried Chicken store. Although his wife's father never liked him, Gacy had married the man's only daughter, and, since he wanted her to live close by, Gacy was given the job.[16] Once in Waterloo, Gacy immediately turned to the Jaycees for social diversion and to advance his status. His wife remembers that he constantly worked, either at the store or with the civic organizations he joined, and he was a great success at both. With the birth of their second child, this time a daughter, the Gacy household seemed idyllic.[17] Something terribly wrong, however, was beginning to take shape. Gacy was becoming adept at braggadocio and lying. He exaggerated about his successes and his importance within the community. In fact, he thought that he was so influential that he could not even pay to get arrested. Moreover, it never appeared to bother him when he was caught in a lie; he simply manufactured another.[18]

Some remember him not as a pillar of the community but as a boastful, arrogant know-it-all who wanted to dominate everyone. They recall that whenever his plans went awry he never admitted fault and always transferred blame to someone else.[19] Gacy also was developing an intense obsession with police equipment and emergency vehicles, the latter of which he often followed at high speed with his own portable red light flashing. He became a member of the local Merchants Patrol, an auxiliary law enforcement group manned by ordinary citizens and designed to supplement police protection of various businesses. While on these patrols, he always carried a handgun and a police radio; he even equipped his station wagon with a makeshift siren.[20] Gacy often took young male employees with him during his night-time "tour of duty." Rather than protect the businesses in town, however, he and his young companions often committed minor thefts. Gacy monitored his police radio for approaching squad cars, while his employees stole petty cash, cans of paint, or auto parts. He later recalled that he had been a petty thief all his life.[21]

Furthermore, Gacy had started boasting to friends of his physical appeal to women and delighted in relating his alleged sexual adventures. In sharp contrast, his relationship with his wife had soured, and friends noted that there were never any public displays of affection. In fact, on several occasions while in his wife's presence, he even offered her sexual favors to other men. He also began displaying a quick temper and erupted in a fit of rage at the slightest mishap. In addition, he became a skilled manipulator of those around him and chose his tactics carefully to suit his purpose. He catered to the community's influential citizens by doing them favors while at the same time promoting himself.[22]

More ominous than this, however, was that Gacy began to invite young men, mostly his employees, to his home for drinks and a game of pool, but his attention turned quickly to sex. When the boys were intoxicated, he then propositioned them. If he was rebuffed, Gacy would use his manipulative talents to convince them to submit. One of these young men was sixteen-year-old Edward Lynch,[23] who worked as a cook for him.

While Gacy's wife was in the hospital delivering their second child, he had persuaded Lynch to accompany him to his house. Once there, the two played pool, and Gacy supplied Lynch with liquor. At one point, Gacy suggested that he perform fellatio on the boy, but Lynch refused. Gacy then threatened him with a carving knife, and a struggle erupted, whereby Lynch received a cut on his arm. Suddenly, Gacy ended the attack and became extremely apologetic. He bandaged the boy's wound and, with his manipulative talents, convinced Lynch to stay with him and view stag films.[24] When the movies were over, Gacy approached Lynch with a chain and padlock. Convincing the boy that he meant no harm, he was able to shackle his hands behind him.

Gacy pushed him face down onto a folding cot and sat on the boy's back, choking him until the youth passed out. Lynch regained consciousness shortly thereafter and found his hands unshackled. Gacy was once again very apologetic. Lynch left the house and was fired from his job a few days later.[25]

A second youth, Donald Vorhees, Jr.,[26] also age sixteen, was assaulted repeatedly by Gacy, who had convinced him that he was doing research on sexual behavior similar to the Kinsey report.[27] Over several months, Gacy forced Vorhees to submit to both oral and anal sex. Eventually, Vorhees told his father about the continual assaults, and Gacy was arrested and charged with sodomy.

At this time, Gacy was ordered to undergo a psychiatric evaluation at the Psychopathic Hospital at the State University of Iowa. A physical examination, including X rays of his internal organs, revealed no evidence of heart disease, nor was he suffering from any form of brain damage. Skull X rays showed no abnormalities, and electroencephalographic readings were normal. In describing Gacy, the doctors reported that he was ingratiating with those in authority but domineering toward those he perceived as weak or submissive. They also concluded that his behavior was more a matter of "thrill seeking" than a fixation on abnormal sexual behavior.[28] He was found competent to stand trial and was diagnosed as having an antisocial personality.[29] Before the trial date was reached, however, Gacy volunteered to submit to a polygraph test to prove his innocence. He took two separate tests, conducted on different dates. With each denial of the charges against him, the polygraph showed that he was lying; Gacy had failed miserably. He then pleaded guilty to the sodomy charges and on December 3, 1968, was sentenced to ten years in the Iowa State Men's Reformatory.[30]

In prison, Gacy adjusted well and became a model of good behavior. He worked in the kitchen and within a matter of months became the number one cook. Once in that position, he exploited the privileges that came with it. Indeed, he enjoyed considerable power at the institution because of his control over the food.[31] He also started a chapter of the Jaycees within the prison, thereby seeming to be a success even while incarcerated. During his imprisonment, however, Gacy's wife filed for and received a divorce. Although visitation rights of his children were left pending, he never saw them again. He told his fellow prisoners that as far as he was concerned they were dead.[32] Another blow to Gacy, which proved to be traumatic, was the death of his father on Christmas Day 1969. Prison officials would not allow him to attend the funeral, and he was upset that, as the last of the remaining males in his immediate family, he could not be there to comfort his mother and sisters.[33]

Gacy was paroled from the Iowa prison on June 18, 1970, just sixteen months after entering the institution, and released to the custody of his mother. At that time, doctors were convinced that the likelihood of further antisocial conduct was small. Eight months later he would be picked up on a disorderly conduct charge resulting from a sexual encounter with a homosexual boy. The charges, however, were dismissed.[34] Gacy and his mother moved back to Chicago, where he found employment as a painter and maintenance worker and eventually became president of his own successful contracting company. He also reestablished an old relationship with Cathy Hull,[35] and they were married in July 1972. By that time, his mother had moved out of the house, and Cathy, with her two daughters from a previous marriage, had moved in.[36] The future for the new family looked bright.

However, the marriage began to decline six months later when late at night Gacy started bringing young men into the garage, where he kept a mattress on the floor. His wife often discovered signs of masturbation and frequently found her bikini underpants in the garage. On one occasion he pointed out to her particular types of young men, with blond hair and a certain shaped rear end, that sexually aroused him. With her, however, he was impotent. In addition, Gacy's temper was beginning to frighten her. He often flew into a fit of rage over the slightest annoyance, sometimes breaking furniture. But as quickly as these outbursts started they stopped, and he was oblivious to the anger he had displayed only moments before.[37] The two were eventually divorced early in 1976.

Later, Gacy's wife recalled the foul odor emanating from the crawl space of the house and how it became increasingly worse. When she complained, her husband had told her that it was caused by the dampness in the ground. The smell, however, became so bad that gnats and other insects were attracted to the house. What she did not realize was that the rancid odor was from the decaying remains of the young men and boys whom Gacy had been methodically killing since 1972 and steadily burying in the crawl space.

Gacy recalled how his first victim had been killed late at night, some time around January 3, 1972. He had picked him up from a Greyhound bus terminal in Chicago and had brought him home, where the two engaged in sex. Afterward, Gacy stabbed the boy to death and buried him in the crawl space. He also relates that he killed a "drag queen" he had picked up off the street. Professing to know magic, Gacy tied a rope around his victim's neck and knotted it. He then twisted it two or three times until the young man convulsed and died.[38]

The killings continued virtually unnoticed until late 1978. If a young boy was reported missing, police merely treated the case as another runaway and told his parents that nothing could be done for twenty-four hours. The father of one missing boy repeatedly urged the police to investigate Gacy, the boy's former employer, but officials assured him that his son was alive because no body had been recovered. Moreover, on at least four occasions, Gacy's name appeared as a suspect or witness in missing boys' cases, yet his association with these youths was never linked together by police.[39]

This failure to recognize Gacy as a common thread in many of these cases can be directly attributed to the procedures of the Chicago Police Department. Lack of communication among various divisions of the police force enabled Gacy to go undetected for many months. For example, the family of one victim reported their son missing to the department's Area Six Division, while another family reported to Area Five.[40] These records were never shared across divisional lines, nor were they collected in a central filing system. Although police staked out Gacy's house in January 1976 in the case of a missing nine-year-old prostitute, no evidence was recovered, and the surveillance was halted after two weeks.[41] Thus, Gacy's repeated connection to missing boys went unnoticed until, on December 11, 1978, fifteen-year-old Robert Piest disappeared after being seen with Gacy, who had been hired to remodel portions of the pharmacy where Piest was a part-time employee. That night Gacy was in the store taking preliminary measurements. He offered the boy a better paying job with his contracting company. Piest was last seen heading toward Gacy's truck around 9:00 P.M.[42]

A full-scale investigation of the boy's disappearance was begun. Gacy became the prime suspect when his past criminal conviction for sodomy was discovered by police, who then conducted a land-and-air search for Piest, based upon Gacy's movements after the disappearance.[43] In addition, a twenty-four-hour surveillance of Gacy was established. Seemingly unconcerned by this attention, Gacy bragged to his neighbors that the police following him were his bodyguards. He became friendly with the officers, often inviting them into his house for drinks or treating them to dinner. While in his home, they noticed the strong foul odor but could not identify it. For his part, Gacy considered the entire police effort a joke. In fact, he delighted in sneaking up behind the officers or leading them on wild chases through the city, often reaching speeds of up to one hundred miles per hour.[44]

By the third day of the investigation, Gacy was linked to four other missing or dead youths. He also was connected to stolen property belonging to one of these young men.[45] Based upon this information a warrant was obtained, and Gacy's house was searched. Inside police discovered drivers' licenses and other forms of identification cards as well as jewelry belonging to several different young men. They also found several sets of handcuffs, a number of police badges, pistols, various mechanical devices for use in sexual intercourse, and a tremendous amount of pornographic material.[46] A cursory examination of the crawl space uncovered nothing, however, as the ground beneath the house appeared undisturbed.

By December 21, 1978, Gacy seemed to be feeling the strain of both the constant surveillance and the mounting evidence against him. Police followed him throughout the Chicago area that day as he visited friends, saying goodbye for what he told them would be the last time. When the officers saw him pass a bag of marijuana to a friend, he was arrested. While Gacy was in custody, one policeman finally realized that the stench from Gacy's crawl space was the same odor he had smelled many times in the county morgue. A second search warrant was obtained, and officers rushed to Gacy's house. What they found there shocked the nation. A total of twenty-six bodies was exhumed from beneath his home. Forensic pathologists and odontologists, physical anthropologists, and radiologists performed the arduous task of identifying the victims one by one.[47]

John Butkovich, age seventeen, who disappeared on July 29, 1975, was an employee of Gacy's. The two had quarreled, right before the young man's disappearance, about money Gacy owed him. He was found buried in the garage with a clothlike material lodged in his throat.

Darryl Samson, age eighteen, was discovered in the crawl space and also had a cloth stuffed down his throat. He had been missing since April 6, 1976. When his mother first notified the police, she was told that he had simply run away.

Samuel Todd Stapleton, age fourteen, disappeared on May 14, 1976, and was last seen by his mother leaving for his sister's house. His chain bracelet was found in Gacy's house. Also, on the afternoon of that same day, Randall Reffett, age fifteen, disappeared, and many believe that he and Stapleton were killed together.

Michael Bonnin, age seventeen, was last seen on June 3, 1976, when he left home with a friend to work on a painting job. Gacy retained Bonnin's fishing license as a souvenir before burying him.

William Carroll, age sixteen, was last seen just before midnight on June 13, 1976. He told his mother that he would be back in one hour, but he never returned.

Sixteen-year-old Rick Johnston disappeared on August 6, 1976, after attending a rock concert, which took place on Chicago's North Side, one mile from Gacy's house.

Seventeen-year-old Gregory J. Godzik, who lived just one mile from Gacy, was hired by him on December 5, 1976. The young man was last seen alive at 1:30 A.M. on December 12 as he left his girlfriend's house on his way to a party.

Nineteen-year-old John A. Szyc was friends with both John Butkovich and Gregory Godzik. Police found his high-school ring in Gacy's house and discovered that Gacy had forged the youth's signature on the title to a 1971 Plymouth and then sold the car to an acquaintance. Szyc was last seen on January 20, 1977, on Chicago's North Side.

Jon Prestidge, age twenty, had just moved to Chicago. He disappeared on March 15, 1977, after leaving a restaurant on the city's North Side.

Matthew H. Bowman, age nineteen, was last seen by his mother on July 5, 1977. She had dropped him off at a suburban Chicago train station.

Robert Gilroy, age twenty-one, left his home, which was only four blocks from Gacy's house, for a horseback riding lesson on September 15, 1977. Since he did not own a car, he sometimes hitchhiked to the Blue Ribbon Stables. He was never seen again.

Nineteen-year-old John Mowery, a former marine, was last seen on September 25, 1977; he had been visiting his mother in Chicago. Borrowing an umbrella from her, he walked into the rainy night and disappeared.

Russel O. Nelson, age twenty, came to Chicago from Minnesota. His future seemed bright as a promising architecture student, and he was planning to marry soon. On October 17, 1977, he failed to return home after leaving a local disco.

On November 10, 1977, sixteen-year-old Robert Winch left his house in Kalamazoo, Michigan, accompanied by a friend. When he failed to return, the police simply classified him as a runaway.

Tommy Boling, age twenty, was last seen on November 18, 1977, at a bar on Chicago's North Side. After telephoning his mother, he told friends that he was headed home to his wife and infant son, but he never made it.

David Paul Talsma, age nineteen, had just completed marine basic training and was home awaiting his assignment. On December 9, 1977, he left his house for a rock concert and disappeared.

William Kindred, another nineteen-year-old, was engaged to be married when he disappeared on February 16, 1978. After leaving his fiancée's apartment, he stopped home briefly and told his roommate that he was going to a bar. The gold religious medallion that his fiancée had given him was found in Gacy's house.

At this point, Gacy relates that there was no more room beneath his house to bury his victims. Moreover, he had already buried one person in the garage and another under his backyard barbecue pit. This did not stop him from killing, however.

Instead of burial, the remaining victims were dumped off the I-55 bridge into the Des Plaines River.

Timothy O'Rourke was last seen leaving his house late one night in mid-June 1978 after telling his roommates that he was going out to buy cigarettes. He was acquainted with Gacy, and the two had discussed the possibility of employment in Gacy's contracting company. His nude body was found floating in the river on June 30, 1978.

Nineteen-year-old Frank W. (Dale) Landingin was last seen on November 4, 1978. The day before he had been released from jail, having posted bond on an assault-and-battery charge. Before his disappearance, he had shared a drink with his father at a bar on Chicago's North Side and then headed on foot toward his girlfriend's house at approximately 3:00 A.M. He was found floating in the river on November 12, 1978, with his own bikini briefs lodged in his throat. The coroner discovered that either the gag itself, or some unbearable external stimuli, caused him to retch and drown in his own vomit.[48] The bail bond slip he had obtained as a receipt was found in Gacy's house.

James Mazzara, age twenty, worked in construction and had a criminal record. He disappeared on Thanksgiving Day 1978. After enjoying dinner with his parents, he returned to his apartment on Chicago's North Side. When he arrived, he discovered that he had been evicted. Last seen walking along the street, alone and with a suitcase, he was found in the river on December 28, 1978, one mile downstream from the I-55 bridge.

Finally, as already noted, Gacy killed Robert Piest on December 11, 1978. The boy died some time between 9:00 and 10:00 P.M., when he was strangled with a rope. After sleeping next to the corpse all night, Gacy stored the body in his attic. That evening he wrapped it in a blanket, placed it in the trunk of his car, and then threw Piest into the Des Plaines River, where he was not recovered until April 9, 1979. A clothlike material was found lodged in the youth's throat. Gacy is also suspected of killing Charles Antonio Hattula, age twenty-seven and one of his employees for a short time. He was found drowned on Mother's Day 1977, in Freeport, Illinois, some seventy miles southwest of Chicago. His death was initially ruled an accident.

The remaining victims unearthed from Gacy's graveyards went unidentified. This may be because they were from out of state, were drifters, or perhaps because their dental and medical records were never sent to the police by parents who simply would not accept that their sons were dead. When buried by authorities, the headstones of the unidentified young men bore the simple inscriptions: "We Are Remembered."[49]

The similarities between Gacy's victims are readily apparent. All were young males, most between the ages of fifteen and twenty. They were slender, muscular, short, and all weighed less than 150 pounds. An overwhelming majority had blue eyes and light-colored hair, either sandy blond, red, or light brown.[50] Some were homosexual, but many were not. They were all killed at Gacy's house, and he claims that they all came there willingly. All but one he murdered by means of a ligature. Many of the victims were found with a paper or clothlike material, usually their own underpants, lodged in their throat. Approximately one half were acquainted with Gacy, having been recently employed by him; the rest were apparently strangers. One was stabbed to death, and at least one was clubbed on the head from behind.

After the first bodies were unearthed, Gacy told police what his life-style had been like for the past several years. He explained that he had developed a fixed schedule for "cruising" for victims. After working until sometimes 10:00 P.M., he slowly drove around Chicago's North Side looking for a teen-age boy with the physical characteristics he liked. Some of the youths he found on the street corner as they sold themselves for money, but many he picked up while they were hitchhiking or simply walking along the roadway.

Dressed in his black leather jacket and displaying a policeman's badge, Gacy would cruise for hours in his black Oldsmobile, which was equipped with a flashing red light, police radio, and siren. Often using the name of Officer Jack Hanley, he was able to capture his victims' attention. Gacy would then either threaten arrest, thereby frightening them into submission, or assure them that he was their friend, someone to rely upon if they were ever in trouble.[51] With both methods, he rarely had any difficulty convincing his victim to get into his car. Once there, his ingratiating manner enabled Gacy to easily persuade the boy to accompany him back to his house, where they usually shared alcoholic drinks and marijuana. In addition, Gacy took pills, mostly Valium.[52]

As these intoxicants took effect, Gacy announced that he knew a few magic tricks, produced a pair of handcuffs, and convinced his victim to put them on. With the youth now helpless, Gacy became cruelly abusive and sexually assaulted him. Afterward, he produced a ligature rope, explaining that this was another magic trick. He then looped the rope around the young man's neck, knotted it twice, placed a hammer handle against the knots, and then knotted it a third time around the handle. Death came when he twisted the handle, thereby tightening the rope like a tourniquet.[53]

On several occasions Gacy sexually assaulted his victims after they were dead; at other times, he stored their bodies under his bed for short periods of time. He told police that he usually had sex with the victim between 1:00 and 3:00 A.M. and that, except for two, all had died between 3:00 and 6:00 A.M. He then buried them in the crawl space under a foot of earth, sometimes one on top of the other. He also related that on two or three evenings he had "doubles" and killed twice in the same night.[54]

Gacy told police that he had murdered either because his victim demanded too much money for sex or posed some sort of threat, such as telling neighbors of Gacy's activities. In his mind, however, those who merely showed remorse after a sexual act also posed a danger. Gacy as well rationalized that he did not kill the boys; rather, he explained that, as he twisted the rope, they began to convulse, thereby making the rope tighter. In this way, "they killed themselves."[55] He was adamant on one point: He was not, he said, a homosexual, and he told investigators that he disliked gays with a passion. He also maintained that he was always intoxicated on pills or alcohol when the murders were committed. Witnesses who talked with Gacy briefly before the murder of Robert Piest, however, stated that Gacy was neither drunk nor on drugs. In fact, he even took two business calls while the boy was dying in front of him, and the men who spoke with him said that he seemed calm and rational.[56]

After his arrest for the murder of Piest, Gacy was examined by several psychiatrists. He related to them that throughout his life he was always looking for acceptance as a successful individual because of the way his father had treated him. He also admitted that from about the time he was sixteen he was constantly thinking of death. When asked why he buried the bodies in his

34   *To Kill Again*

crawl space, he stated that they were his "property," sometimes
referring to them as his "trophies." It was a source of pride for
him, and he enjoyed informing the doctors that he was in the
Guinness Book of World Records, explaining that a person does not
get into that book by being "dumb and stupid." When further
questioned about why he experienced no remorse for his crimes,
he simply noted that he was trying to understand why he had
committed these acts and was too confused to feel sorry for what
he had done.[57]

When the examinations were completed, several psychiatrists gave varying diagnoses. Gacy was described by one as
egocentric, narcissistic, antisocial, and exploitative. Another
concluded that he exhibited a psychopathic personality, with
episodes of paranoid schizophrenia, the latter as the severest,
although not the dominant, part of the illness. He showed no
evidence of any organic brain disease, and his attempt to convince
psychiatrists of a split personality failed miserably. Moreover,
doctors found that he had no physical illness of any magnitude.
As for his earlier fainting spells, it was believed that these were
brought on by anxiety.[58] Although he was intelligent, with an IQ
of 118, it was thought that he had not developed emotionally
much past the level of an infant. He had a great need to be loved
and admired, was charming on the outside but cold and ruthless
underneath, and had a clear absence of any feelings of guilt.[59]

The psychiatrists surmised that Gacy's crimes were an expression of aggression, rather than the sexual drive, in which he
sought to degrade, punish, and humiliate his victims by gaining
power and control over them. This behavioral pattern explains
why he slept with the corpses of some of his victims, for, in such
a state, they were completely helpless. It was also believed that
the boys chosen as victims represented what Gacy had never
been able to attain. He had been a flabby and physically unfit
youth while these boys were muscular and trim; they personified
what he had failed to achieve.[60]

To those around him, John Gacy appeared to be a man of
boundless energy, both physical and mental. In fact, his second
wife related that he rarely slept more than two hours per night,
and a former employee described him as a perfectionist.[61] Indeed,
he was meticulously neat in his housekeeping, so much so that,
when police were exhuming bodies from his crawl space, he was

more concerned with the mud being left on his rugs than with the charges that were mounting against him. Those who knew him say that he always seemed to be striving for a state of social grace that he could never quite attain. Throughout the investigation of the murders, Gacy believed that he would never be convicted, and, when confessing to police, he spoke with an air of confidence and security.[62] He still maintains that attitude today, sure that the twelve death sentences imposed upon him will never be carried out.[63]

Notes

1. Sullivan and Maiken at 23–24, 70, 242.
2. Id. at 214.
3. Linedecker at 11.
4. Id. at 17.
5. Cahill at 33.
6. Id. at 34; Egger at 162.
7. Cahill at 35.
8. Egger at 162.
9. Sullivan and Maiken at 235–36.
10. Id. at 237.
11. Linedecker at 18; Sullivan and Maiken at 237; Egger at 162.
12. Cahill at 39.
13. Id. at 47; Linedecker at 19.
14. Cahill at 365.
15. Sullivan and Maiken at 237–38, 236.
16. Cahill at 54.
17. Linedecker at 25, 24.
18. Cahill at 57; Linedecker at 26.
19. Sullivan and Maiken at 242.
20. Id. at 241; Cahill at 56; Linedecker at 27.
21. Sullivan and Maiken at 241; Cahill at 75, 28.
22. Sullivan and Maiken at 241, 243, 242.
23. This person is identified as Edward Lynch in Sullivan and Maiken and in Cahill, and as James Tullery in Linedecker. The name Edward Lynch will be used in this book.
24. Cahill at 66–68.
25. Id. at 68–70; Linedecker at 31.
26. This person is identified as Donald Vorhees, Jr., in Sullivan and Maiken and in Cahill, and as Mark Miller in Linedecker. The name Donald Vorhees, Jr., will be used in this book.
27. See Linedecker at 31–32; Cahill at 61, 84.
28. Cahill at 86–88, 89.
29. Sullivan and Maiken at 249.
30. Cahill at 70, 73; Sullivan and Maiken at 250.

31. Cahill at 94.
32. Sullivan and Maiken at 251–52.
33. Linedecker at 47.
34. Cahill at 99; Sullivan and Maiken at 253–54.
35. This person is identified as Cathy Hull in Sullivan and Maiken and as Carol Lofgren in Cahill. The name Cathy Hull will be used in this book.
36. Sullivan and Maiken at 255; Cahill at 120.
37. Sullivan and Maiken at 66–67; Linedecker at 66.
38. Sullivan and Maiken at 163.
39. Egger at 199, 198.
40. Cahill at 186.
41. Egger at 199.
42. Sullivan and Maiken at 5.
43. Egger at 197.
44. Sullivan and Maiken at 69, 59.
45. Egger at 197.
46. Sullivan and Maiken at 28–29.
47. Egger at 179, 198.
48. Cahill at 233.
49. Id. at 230; Sullivan and Maiken at 214.
50. Cahill at 207.
51. Sullivan and Maiken at 163–64.
52. Cahill at 179.
53. Id. at 313; Sullivan and Maiken at 161.
54. Sullivan and Maiken at 162, 206, 164, 161.
55. Id. at 206–7.
56. Cahill at 235.
57. Id. at 39–40, 368–69, 184.
58. Sullivan and Maiken at 231–33.
59. Id. at 249, 325, 233.
60. Cahill at 336, 328–29.
61. Linedecker at 65; Sullivan and Maiken at 62.
62. Sullivan and Maiken at 28, 173, 189, 218, 161.
63. Simon at 29-A.

3 Profile of the Serial Murderer

The life-styles and personalities of Theodore Bundy and John Gacy share many common features. The development of their personal lives and the patterns of crimes that they ultimately committed are frighteningly similar. When compared with other serial murderers, it is apparent that Bundy and Gacy are not unique; indeed, many serial killers possess these same behavioral and developmental traits. By compiling and assessing these common characteristics, a clear profile emerges of the typical serial murderer, thereby providing a better understanding of how such an individual appears to the rest of society.

The early home life of many serial killers is often one in which a stable, nurturing atmosphere is sorely lacking. Most come from broken families or homes where they were physically or psychologically abused. As seen in Chapter 2, Gacy's father was a drunkard who regularly beat his wife and belittled his son. The young Gacy found that he could do nothing right and could never please his father. Similarly, Gerald Stano, who confessed to the murder of at least twenty-five young women in Florida and is linked to almost forty such killings, was the fifth child of a mother who lost all of her children to adoption because she abused and neglected them. They were so badly mistreated that, at the time Gerald was removed from his home, for instance, he was malnourished, physically and emotionally neglected, and was functioning at an "animalistic" level. Although saved from the abuses of his natural mother, Stano's adoptive parents inflicted their own degree of corporal punishment. His mother disciplined him with a ruler, his father with a razor strop. Most of the time his mother dominated the household, and she did so with an iron hand.[1]

Albert DeSalvo, who terrorized women in 1962–63 as the famed Boston Strangler, was victim to both the Boston slums and his father's outrage. He suffered a childhood of deprivation and was tyrannized by a violent and alcoholic father who abused his wife and six children.[2] On one occasion, Stano watched in horror as his mother's fingers were broken one by one. By the time he was five years old, the elder DeSalvo was already teaching his son how to shoplift. Later in his youth his father sold both his sister and him as slaves to a local farmer. This enslavement lasted for several months.[3]

Edmund Kemper, who murdered six young women in California in 1972–73, was a child of divorced parents, who, when they were together, fought violently, usually over how young Edmund should be raised. After his father abandoned the family, his mother dominated the boy, often mistreating him. When he was ten years old, she locked him in the basement each night, forcing him to sleep there for eight months. Kemper's childhood was a frightening and miserable time, one of loneliness and confusion at not being able to please his demanding mother.[4] He later explained that he always felt as though he were nothing more than "a puppet on a string," being manipulated by his mother, who tormented and laughed at him while she was in one of her drunken stupors.[5] She continued this abuse until the day she was killed, when he beheaded her.

Dean Arnold Corll, Elmer Wayne Henley, and David Owen Brooks together sexually assaulted and murdered twenty-seven young boys in Houston, Texas, over a three-year period. Each one grew up in either a fatherless home or in an environment in which they suffered repeated brutalization by a father who was either inconsistent regarding discipline or unpredictably violent.[6]

Henry Lee Lucas and Ottis Elwood Toole are believed to have killed at least 199 people in twenty-seven states between August 1975 and June 1983.[7] Lucas was born poor in rural Virginia to a prostitute and grew up in squalor, often having to steal his own food and eat off the floor.[8] He lived in a two-room dirt-floor cabin with his mother, a man he remembers as his father (although records indicate that this man was not his natural father), his older brother, and his mother's boyfriend. Because his father was disabled and an alcoholic, Lucas's mother was the head of the family and was extremely domineering. From ages four to seven, she dressed her son in female clothing, allowing his hair to grow long and treating him as though he were a girl. When his hair was finally cut, he claims that his mother began to beat him, made him carry heavy objects, steal, cut wood, carry water, and "attend to the hog."[9] She also forced him to watch her have sexual intercourse with the various men she enticed for payment.[10] Lucas claims that he never had fun as a child and that, if he even tried, his mother would beat him. He bears a scar on the back of his head that he says is the result of a blow delivered by his mother with a two-by-four.[11]

Toole, eleven years younger than Lucas, grew up with an alcoholic father and a mother who suffered from mental illness. As a child, he set fires and often ran away from home. He also dressed in girls' clothing but, contrary to Lucas, liked to do so. Throughout his life he was very attached to his mother. After her death in 1981, he often went to her grave to lie on top of it.[12]

Norman Collins, who murdered seven young women in Michigan and one in California between 1967 and 1969, also suffered at the hands of an abusive alcoholic. His mother was married three times, and the last of her husbands was a chronic drunkard who beat her and the children regularly. The daily scene was one of recriminations, denunciations, angry blows, furniture upended, and terrified children screaming in panic.[13]

Kenneth Bianchi, the Hillside Strangler, who, together with his cousin Angelo Buono, killed as many as thirteen young women in Los Angeles between October 1977 and February 1978,[14] also endured a very unhappy childhood. His early life was spent in foster homes, where he was sent by his teenage mother when she ran out of relatives to care for him. Eventually, he was adopted by a seemingly stable and caring couple from Rochester, New York.[15] Contrary to this outward appearance, there is some evidence that his adoptive mother physically abused him, beating him with a belt and holding his hand over a flame.[16] However, most of the abuse inflicted upon Bianchi was psychological. His adoptive mother was a domineering woman who held strong control over the young child.[17] She was extremely overprotective and was deeply disturbed by the fact that she could not bear children of her own. She constantly took Bianchi to doctors for a host of different illnesses, most notably a lingering problem with enuresis, or involuntary urination. Frequently these illnesses were diagnosed as psychosomatic in nature, and, when doctors suggested that both she and Bianchi seek psychiatric help, she always refused.[18]

Ted Bundy, as seen in Chapter 1, was born out of wedlock and never knew his real father. Although his adoptive father was not abusive, Bundy was scornful of him. A nurturing relationship therefore never developed between them, leaving the family with a lack of strength and continuity.

Finally, David Berkowitz, who held New York City in his grips as the Son of Sam, or the .44 Caliber Killer, was likewise born illegitimately to a woman who believed that she could not raise him. As a result, he was given up for adoption when he was only a few days old. As a child, Berkowitz was told that his natural mother had died while giving birth, and for many years he suffered from intense feelings of guilt because he believed that he was somehow responsible. When he discovered that she was actually still alive and had willingly placed him up for adoption, he was devastated by her rejection. Although his adoptive parents were never abusive, Berkowitz was ambivalent toward them.[19] They indulged him by granting his every wish yet frequently criticized him. He eventually found that he could never quite meet their high standards. In time, he also grew to dislike his father because of the jealousy the younger Berkowitz harbored for his mother.[20]

An exhaustive study conducted by the Federal Bureau of Investigation confirms that most serial killers spent their childhoods in unhealthy, uncaring, and abusive homes; a wholesome, nurturing environment was rarely seen.[21] After interviewing numerous convicted serial murderers throughout the United States, members of the FBI's Behavioral Sciences Unit selected thirty-six men as a representative sample and conducted an in-depth analysis of these men. They found that their family histories were highlighted by multiple problems, including alcohol and drug abuse, and by sexual difficulties among family members. The researchers further noted that these men reported unfair, hostile, inconsistent, and frequently abusive discipline. It was concluded that, while growing up, most of the thirty-six murderers had weak attachments to family members and had parents who, while suffering from problems of substance abuse, criminality, and aberrant sexual behavior, offered role models for deviant conduct.[22]

Complicating this already unhappy existence, some serial murderers suffered from a physical injury or handicap while they were young. Gacy was a sickly child who suffered from fainting spells, which doctors later attributed to a blood clot on the brain caused by a playground accident. Bianchi, who was prone to falls, similarly experienced a playground injury as a child when he fell from a jungle gym at school, striking the back of his head. Soon thereafter he began having petit mal seizures.[23] Furthermore, there was his continuing problem with enuresis. And, after being hit in the head with a two-by-four, Lucas reportedly was in a semiconscious state for three days. Subsequently, he suffered from frequent dizziness, blackouts, and at times felt as if he were "floating."[24] It is believed that he sustained serious trauma to portions of his brain. Interestingly, however, doctors in both the Gacy and Bianchi cases later attributed their physical maladies to psychological causes and not to physical injury.

As a result of their childhood experiences, serial killers never seem to develop a sense of self-worth. Bundy was extremely shy, to the point of being introverted, and he had very little self-confidence. Likewise, a healthy self-esteem was conspicuously absent from Berkowitz's personality,[25] and Lucas was virtually incapacitated by an inferiority complex and lacked self-confidence, self-reliance, will power, and general stamina.[26] Consequently, many serial killers tend to avoid contact with other people, and they spend much of their childhood alone. Most, including Bianchi, Gacy, and Berkowitz, were considered "loners" by those who knew them.[27] This character trait remains with them in adulthood.

Serial killers often turn to fantasy during their childhood as a way to break free from an unpleasant environment, and this daydreaming eventually becomes an important part of their everyday existence. However, these are not fantasies of escape to a better life but rather are of aggression, mastery, and domination over others.[28] Berkowitz has related how he was obsessed with death and fantasized about it from early childhood because it has a wonderful power.[29] Gacy as well dwelt upon death from an early age. And, as a child, Kemper often thought about killing individuals and groups. As part of his fantasy, he cut off the heads and hands of his sister's dolls. When he was eight years old he revealed to his sister that he had a crush on one of his teachers and wished to kiss her. His sister encouraged him to do so, but he replied that he would have to kill the teacher first.[30] Similarly, Bundy turned to fantasy in childhood as a relief from what he perceived to be his "stultifyingly middle-class" background.

Perhaps because serial murderers were never exposed to a close, loving relationship as children, they are incapable of developing any lasting and meaningful relationships as adults. They suffer from a severe inability to interact socially as well as sexually. FBI Special Agent Robert Ressler maintains that serial killers usually never have a satisfactory relationship with any person in their lives. They shun close attachments because they are afraid of any possible failure in life. Indeed, Kemper has explained that he was "emotionally impotent" and that he was terribly frightened of failing at male-female relationships.[31] This inability to form close personal attachments was present not only in Bundy's life with his adoptive father, Meg Anders, and Stephanie Brooks but also in Gacy's with the women he married. In Stano's case, psychiatrists noted that throughout his life he was never able to have a normal relationship with a woman and, in general, did not interact well with people.[32]

Fueled by the frustration of their inability to experience social and sexual relationships and their exposure to abuse and neglect as children, serial killers' fantasies eventually center upon sex and violence.[33] They become fascinated with pornography and sadistic sexual behavior. This was seen with both Bundy and Gacy, and it also was evident with Bianchi, who, as a teenager, was a frequent purchaser of hard-core pornography.[34] When he was arrested, police discovered numerous pornographic movies in Bianchi's home, in addition to a briefcase filled with sex books, several pairs of semen-stained undershorts, and a large semen-stained towel.[35] This obsession with pornographic material acts as an aid in the construction of the serial murderer's elaborate fantasy world, and soon his fantasized sexual encounters replace any attempt for actual interpersonal relationships, at which he has been so unsuccessful. The imaginary world that thus emerges plays an important role in the crimes that the serial killer ultimately commits since, after the first murder, the memory of the act stimulates and contributes to the fantasies of subsequent murders. Indeed, he finds himself preoccupied with his fantasies of sex and violence as they intensify with each succeeding crime.[36]

In most instances these fantasies are hidden from the rest of society as the serial murderer presents to his friends and family a facade of normalcy. Most who know him consider him to be affable and pleasant. Corll was a scoutmaster and a church youth director, who gave the impression of a "clean-cut man who loved children." An acquaintance of Corll's even remarked that he was "the nicest person you'll ever meet."[37] To a Texas neighbor, Lucas "seemed like an ordinary person, real polite and real nice." Bianchi as well was described by a friend as a nice young man.[38] When he was arrested, his live-in girlfriend stated emphatically that he could never have hurt anyone since he simply was not that kind of person.[39] The same reaction also was evident with the families and friends of Bundy, Gacy, and Berkowitz.

The serial murderer thus appears to others as a normal, healthy individual. There is no sign of overt mental illness, and psychosis is rarely present.[40] He is not delusional nor does he suffer from hallucinations; in fact, he is "extraordinarily ordinary."[41] He is articulate and ingratiating and is often considered charming and charismatic. With these qualities he is successfully able to control those around him and to use these manipulative talents to obtain whatever he seeks. For instance, Bundy and Gacy both were able to persuade their victims to accompany them. It has been said of Berkowitz that he has an innocent face that can fool anyone and is above suspicion. In fact, Berkowitz himself has explained that "my face, my lips, and my blue eyes are like weapons which I sometimes use to my own advantage."[42] However, when they are unable to get their own way, many serial murderers are prone to violent outbursts of temper. Quite often their moods, such as with Gacy, are erratic and unpredictable. Also, Bianchi's neighbors at times heard him throwing heavy objects against the walls of his apartment.[43]

Another common trait is that many serial killers are usually quite intelligent. Bundy's IQ was measured at 124, Gacy's at 118, Bianchi's between 106 and 116, Berkowitz's between 115 and 118, and Kemper's at 136.[44] Similarly, Wayne Williams, convicted of two murders and suspected of killing at least twenty young black children in Atlanta, was considered brilliant as a child by those who knew him.[45] In contrast to this is Coral Eugene Watts, suspected of murdering at least forty young women in Canada, Michigan, and Texas. He has a reported IQ of 75,[46] well below the average level. Yet, Watts was able to outwit law enforcement authorities for nine years.

The serial killer is perceived by most as successful and promising in both his academic and professional life. Gacy was seen as an accomplished businessman and Bundy as an up-and-coming young attorney. Similarly, Christopher Wilder maintained a prosperous construction company and successful auto-racing team. When he was killed by police in a shoot-out near the Canadian border in April 1984, he was suspected of assaulting or killing at least ten young women in several states.[47]

Despite this outward appearance of success, serial murderers often have a mediocre and even poor performance record in past endeavors. In fact, the FBI's study revealed that, although intelligent, the performance of these killers did not match their potential in academics, employment, sexual relationships, and military service. The bureau's findings indicated that many of these men had to repeat elementary grades, with the majority never finishing high school. Indeed, academic failure was frequently mentioned by the men as having contributed to their overall sense of inadequacy. In addition, most possessed the ability to perform highly skilled jobs yet had poor work histories as unskilled laborers, with only 20 percent ever holding a steady job.[48] To mask this pattern of failure the serial murderer becomes adept at fabrication and braggadocio. As with Gacy and Bundy, they begin to live a life of deceit in order to appear successful. In fact, acquaintances often relate how such individuals seem to be striving for acceptance by everyone around them.

Serial murderers also are often self-centered and feel a great need for attention from others, so much so that, when finally caught, they relish the publicity given to their crimes. When law enforcement officials first questioned Williams about the Atlanta killings, he called a press conference to announce that he was the "prime suspect" in the case.[49] Similarly, both Bundy and Gacy held numerous press conferences from their respective prison cells. After police arrested Paul Knowles, he smiled at everyone and was pleased with the identity that the investigation had given him. Over a four-month period in late 1974, he had killed at least eighteen people, and perhaps as many as thirty-five, in a seven-state area.[50] Lucas also enjoys his celebrity status; in fact, he still grants interviews to journalists from all over the country, thriving upon the attention. Likewise, Kemper continues to receive satisfaction from his status as a multiple murderer.[51]

Almost all known serial killers are between the ages of twenty and thirty-five when they commit their crimes. Although not hardened criminals, most frequently participate in minor crimes, such as Bundy, who regularly shoplifted, and Gacy, who stole auto parts. Likewise, Bianchi took various items from several homes that he was supposed to be protecting as a security guard. Collins as well made a habit of theft and burglary, stealing motorcycle parts and breaking into student dormitory rooms.[52] In this way, serial murderers are preoccupied with obtaining and possessing material things, a condition that remains with them throughout their lives. This is apparent in their later crimes as most retain some item belonging to or associated with their victims. Gacy kept identification cards and jewelry; Bundy and Stano kept much of their victims' clothing. Kemper also held onto clothing as well as books or other personal articles that his victims were carrying.[53] These souvenirs serve as important reminders to the killer of his murderous acts.

Furthermore, it is interesting to note that serial murderers are fascinated and even obsessed with police work, uniforms, and apparatus. Gacy equipped his car with lights and sirens and dressed like a policeman, even carrying a badge and gun. Bundy worked as a college security guard at one time and carried both a policeman and fireman's badge. Berkowitz was a volunteer fireman as well as an auxiliary policeman.[54] Williams was known as a "police groupie" by his friends, and Bianchi pretended to be an undercover highway patrolman, carrying handcuffs and a phony badge and identification card.[55] He also worked as a private security guard and joined a local sheriff's reserve force. Similarly, Stano often told people that he was an undercover policeman.[56] And Kemper equipped his car with a two-way radio, mounted a microphone on the dashboard, and installed a whip antenna on the outside. In addition, he frequently spent time at a bar that catered predominantly to police officers.[57]

Although obsessed with police equipment, most serial killers, however, regard individual officers and police departments as incompetent and bungling. They are usually convinced that they will never be caught or, if apprehended, convicted of their crimes. Lucas has little regard for almost all law enforcement personnel, stating that he has seen "kids play cops" better than the police officials who interviewed him. Both Bundy and Gacy maintained this attitude, as evidenced by the delight they took in playing games with police surveillance teams. Williams as well enjoyed leading police on wild high-speed chases simply for fun.[58]

Serial murderers are also quite often extremely energetic and require little sleep. Furthermore, they are usually meticulously neat in their housekeeping and personal appearance, a quality shared by Bundy, Gacy, Williams, and DeSalvo. And, in every aspect of their lives, they exhibit a strong need to dominate others.[59] Both Gacy and Bundy, through their manipulations, controlled the significant people in their lives, with Bundy even insisting on conducting portions of his own defense. Berkowitz as well was determined to control himself and those around him. The notes he left at the murder scenes were not only meant to taunt the police by challenging their authority and ability to capture him, but also they fueled the fears of the public and cleverly manipulated the news media.[60] Kemper and DeSalvo both committed their crimes because of the power and control they experienced as they held their victims captive and the women submitted to their demands.[61] Lucas's crimes also were the result of his exaggerated need to feel powerful and important. In fact, FBI researchers found that this "intense desire to be strong, powerful, and in control becomes an obsession to dominate through aggression."[62]

Many serial killers, including Gacy and Stano, drink alcohol or use drugs prior to their crimes. Bundy, for instance, explained that the effect of alcohol was an important trigger that helped him commit murder, since his inhibitions were significantly diminished.[63] Similarly, Lucas claims he drank prior to most of his killings, and he still boasts of having kept himself awake with amphetamines, marijuana, or PCP in order to travel all day and night. This use of alcohol also is reflected in the FBI's findings.[64]

Like Lucas, both Bundy and Gacy, as well as almost all serial murderers, spend countless hours driving in search of their victims. Williams, too, constantly drove around Atlanta late at night while monitoring a police scanner, and Berkowitz devoted considerable time to stalking his prey, explaining that this was an important part of his ritual. Some serial murderers confine their prowlings to one specific area, such as Gacy in Chicago and, in southern California, Kemper, who spent most of his evenings and every weekend cruising the freeways for attractive female hitchhikers,[65] and Juan Corona, who murdered twenty-five men over a six-week period in 1971. Others, however, move from state to state, killing as they work their way across the country. Lucas and Toole regularly crisscrossed the nation during their murder sprees, living out of their car and randomly picking up victims of either sex and any race or age. Knowles, in this same seemingly haphazard manner, killed both men and women of all ages in Florida, Ohio, Nevada, Alabama, Connecticut, Virginia, Georgia, and possibly several other states. Similarly, Wilder was wanted by authorities in Florida, Texas, Colorado, and Kansas, as well as in Newcastle, Australia. As the murderers continue their search, they feel a sense of mounting anxiety. Kemper explained that he was under a terrible tension both before and during a kill, a behavioral pattern also experienced by Bundy.[66]

Most of the victims of serial killers are picked up off the street. They are usually prostitutes, hitchhikers, travelers in distress, or simply innocent individuals who happen to be walking along the roadside. Lucas and Toole used this method, as did Kemper and Collins.[67] Many victims, however, are enticed by promises or coerced by threats, both of which were used by Gacy. Corll, Henley, and Brooks invited their victims, mostly teen-age runaways, to paint- and glue-sniffing parties at Corll's house, where they were tortured, sexually assaulted, and then shot or strangled. Bianchi and Buono lured their victims into a van by posing as police officers.[68] Thus, many serial killers seem to follow a pattern of selecting their prey based upon their victims' perceived vulnerability.

Furthermore, rarely do serial murderers know their victims personally, and, if so, it is only a casual or short-term acquaintance. Kemper related that he never even asked their names because he did not want to know who they were.[69] In this way, it was easier for him to see these women as objects rather than as human beings. Each killer's victims are usually of the same sex, age, and physical makeup, and each normally focuses on one type of individual, seeking out someone fitting that preconceived appearance,[70] as in the case of both Gacy and Bundy. Corll, for instance, insisted that his two accomplices only bring young teen-age boys to his home. When a girl was brought to the house, he was so enraged that he threatened Henley and Brooks with their lives. Ultimately, he was killed in the resulting argument.[71] Stano's victims were almost always wearing blue when they died; Collins and Kemper both sought out young attractive college women; and Corona chose only vagrants and migrant workers.[72]

Once a victim is located, most serial murderers wait until they have complete control over the person before striking. Although several women were attacked by Bundy as they slept, he usually killed them after they were in his car, as did Stano. Gacy did not commit his murderous acts until his intended prey was within his home. Likewise, Henley, Brooks, and Corll carried out their crimes only after they were in Corll's house.[73] Most of these murders were committed at night or in the early morning hours by using a hands-on method, such as strangulation, stabbing, or bludgeoning,[74] which affords the serial killer further control over his already helpless victim. There are exceptions, however. Berkowitz, for instance, shot his victims with a .44-caliber revolver, although he turned to guns only after his attempts at murder with a knife had failed,[75] and Lucas and Stano both used firearms at varying times.

Serial murderers usually take their victims' lives one by one. However, sometimes two are killed at once, or what Gacy called "doubles." In other reported cases, Corll killed two young boys at a time on several different occasions between 1970 and 1973. Bundy as well attacked and killed two women on the same day when he abducted both from Lake Sammamish, and Knowles also murdered twice in a twenty-four-hour period.[76] Some serial killers sexually assault their victims before murdering them, but many wait until after death. Gacy, for example, sometimes sexually attacked his victims after they died as well as before, and Lucas has plainly admitted that he is a necrophiliac, explaining that most of the time he had sex with those he killed only after death because otherwise he could not reach sexual satisfaction.[77] Kemper also had sexual intercourse with several of his women victims only after they were dead. Until then, however, he was careful not to assault them sexually. Indeed, while struggling with one woman, stabbing her repeatedly, the back of his hand happened to brush against one of her breasts. Upset and embarrassed, Kemper apologized for having touched her there. It is believed that Stano, too, sexually assaulted his victims after their deaths.[78]

As with Bundy, the serial murderer's first attempts at killing are often bungled and unsuccessful. However, he quickly learns from his mistakes, and taking lives becomes easier and easier. As the murders continue, they intensify in violence, and the killer comes more and more out in the open, taking further chances each time. Toward the end of his killing spree, Kemper severed the head of one of his victims directly outside the picture window of his mother's house. One of the last people murdered by Collins was stabbed and bludgeoned so severely that it appeared as though he was in a "killing frenzy" at the time.[79] The murders also seem to take place more frequently, as the number of days between each steadily decreases.[80]

In disposing of their victims' bodies, most serial killers leave them in wooded areas or in gullies along the roadside, but some, such as Gacy, bury their victims. FBI researchers explain that one reason for hiding or burying the bodies is so that the killer can keep his secret. On the other hand, by displaying the corpse, he is hoping to incite shock and offend society. Each method provides a means of control over the public. Still others dispose of the parts, after mutilating and dismembering their victims. Once a murder is completed, the serial killer experiences a sense of calmness and relaxation, something on the verge of euphoria, becoming completely relaxed.[81]

As the crimes progress the serial killer is driven by an ever-increasing need to murder. As one individual interviewed by the FBI research team explained, "It is a development . . . getting tired of a certain level of fantasy and then going even farther and even more bizarre."[82] Kemper has likened this need to an addiction to drugs or alcohol, stating that "a little isn't enough. . . . The more you get, the more you want."[83] The case histories of both Bundy and Gacy seem to bear this out. Levin and Fox also indicate that the serial killer progressively requires more and more perversity in order to satisfy his needs.[84] This increasing impulse to kill contributes to his heightened exposure as well as to his chances of being caught.

Capture of the serial murderer is often difficult, since at most of the crime scenes he is meticulously careful about not leaving any clues as to his identity. Both Bundy and Gacy left no indication of their involvement; likewise, Stano erased all traces of his actions by faithfully scrubbing the interior of his car after each woman had been murdered. When his vehicle was impounded and analyzed by police, no blood or hair samples were found. Although Watts confessed to the slaying of numerous women in two states, he was not tried for any of them. Instead, he plead guilty to charges of burglary with the intent to commit murder, since authorities were unable to find any proof connecting him to the crimes.[85] With Bianchi and Buono, no sign of the assailants was left where the bodies were discovered. In fact, the police could not even determine where the women had been killed. Similarly, no clues have been found linking Lucas to any crime scene.[86]

Once a serial killer is caught, psychiatrists often label him a sociopath or antisocial personality. Levin and Fox concur with this diagnosis, noting that he is an individual who lacks feelings of guilt, has no conscience, and exhibits an excessive need to control others. He shows no remorse or regret for the acts he has committed and feels no emotion or pity for his victims. Rather, they are nothing more than "life-size dolls" or objects to be used and then cast away. Lucas relates that he went from one victim to the next, never thinking about the last one he killed.[87]

In general, serial murderers seem unable to benefit from experience and are emotionally immature, having never learned to control their violent impulses.[88] They usually disavow any responsibility for their crimes, either by outright denial or by blaming their actions on others, such as Gacy, who faulted the deaths of his victims on the young men themselves. Berkowitz initially claimed that a 6,000-year-old demon had commanded him to kill.[89] Likewise, Bianchi tried to convince psychiatrists that he suffered from multiple personalities, one of which committed the crimes. Both of these attempts were later proven to be clever ploys. In addition, although he originally confessed to numerous murders, Lucas now argues that he is innocent of all charges and is contesting the several convictions against him.[90]

The serial killer is obviously a distinctive and extremely dangerous criminal. He possesses a superficial charm, whereby he may effectively mimic appropriate socially approved behavior in any given setting, but, behind this carefully constructed facade, he exhibits no genuine feelings and is insensitive to the welfare of others. Such an individual usually is viewed by the courts as evil and not insane, since he fully understands the wrongfulness of his conduct and the consequences of his continued acts. Indeed, most observers recognize that the serial killer commits these acts of murder purely for his own pleasure, at the expense of his victims.[91]

Notes

1. Bockman and Taylor at 1A–4A.
2. Frank at 228.
3. Leyton at 113, 131.
4. Cheney at 8, 11.
5. From an interview with Edmund Kemper conducted for the film *Murder: No Apparent Motive.*
6. Olsen at 200–33; Cartel at 109–13; "The Mind of the Mass Murderer" at 56–57.
7. Egger at 247.
8. Stanley at 47; Egger at 253–54; Norris and Birnes at 107.
9. Egger at 251, 253; Norris and Birnes at 107–8.
10. Egger at 252; Cartel at 250; Norris and Birnes at 108.
11. Egger at 253.
12. MacDonald at 161.
13. Keyes at 229–31; Wilson and Seaman at 50.
14. O'Brien at xi; Egger at 202; "Murderous Personality: Was the Hillside Strangler a Jekyll and Hyde?" at 26 (hereafter "Murderous Personality").
15. Schwartz at 119–20, 239–40; Cartel at 155.
16. Schwartz at 195–96; Fisher at 10.
17. Schwartz at 124–30; MacDonald at 215.
18. Schwartz at 123–24; Egger at 200–201.
19. Abrahamsen (1985) at 80, 16, 71, 19.
20. Id. at 201, 49, 45.
21. See the *Federal Bureau of Investigation Law Enforcement Bulletin*, August 1985 (hereafter FBI-August 1985).
22. Id. at 3–4.
23. Schwartz at 123; Egger at 209.
24. Norris and Birnes at 109.
25. Abrahamsen (1985) at 49.

26. Norris and Birnes at 111.
27. "Murderous Personality" at 26; Sullivan and Maiken at 78; Abrahamsen (1985) at 167.
28. FBI-August 1985 at 4.
29. Abrahamsen (1985) at 29–31, 88.
30. Cheney at 9–10.
31. From the film *Murder: No Apparent Motive.*
32. Bockman and Taylor at 4A.
33. FBI-August 1985 at 4.
34. Schwartz at 207; Egger at 205.
35. Schwartz at 148–50; Egger at 206.
36. FBI-August 1985 at 4.
37. Olsen at 226, 133.
38. Stanley at 47; Fisher at 11.
39. Egger at 214; Schwartz at 111–13.
40. From the film *Murder: No Apparent Motive.*
41. Levin and Fox at 48, 229–30; Egger at 13–14; Wilson (Paul) at 51–52.
42. Abrahamsen (1985) at 43.
43. O'Brien at 92; "Murderous Personality" at 26.
44. Rule at 188; Sullivan and Maiken at 249; O'Brien at 89; Fisher at 10; Abrahamsen (1985) at 37, 149; MacDonald at 175.
45. McGrath and Smith at 23.
46. Peer and Shapiro at 29; Cartel at 230–32.
47. Strasser et al. at 38; Lamar at 26.
48. FBI-August 1985 at 4.
49. McGrath and Smith at 23.
50. Wilson and Seaman at 128.
51. Egger at 263; Norris and Birnes at 119; Cheney at 181; Leyton at 68.
52. Shryock at 2; Holmes and DeBurger (1988) at 21; O'Brien at 201–2; Cartel at 165; Keyes at 216; Wilson and Seaman at 49.
53. Shryock at 2; Cheney at 177; Leyton at 65.
54. Abrahamsen (1985) at 60.
55. McGrath and Smith at 23; O'Brien at 149–51; "Murderous Personality" at 26.
56. O'Brien at 200; Egger at 203, 207; Bockman and Taylor at 4A.
57. Cheney at 40–41, 38. See also *Murder: No Apparent Motive.*
58. Egger at 257; McGrath and Smith at 23.
59. Levin and Fox at 229.
60. Abrahamsen (1985) at 19, 4.
61. Cheney at 176; Leyton at 52–53, 137; Frank at 240.
62. Egger at 256; FBI-August 1985 at 5.
63. Bockman and Taylor at 4A; Winn and Merrill at 119–20, 121–22; Leyton at 94.
64. Egger at 250, 267; FBI-August 1985 at 9.
65. McGrath and Smith at 23; Abrahamsen (1985) at 93; Cheney at 41.
66. Wilson and Seaman at 125–28; Strasser et al. at 38; Lamar at 26; Leyton at 68.
67. Keyes at 166–67; Wilson and Seaman at 46–49.
68. Olsen at 156–57; Wilson and Seaman at 55; "The Mind of the Mass Murderer" at 56; O'Brien at 148–55.

69. Levin and Fox at 231. See also *Murder: No Apparent Motive.*

70. FBI-August 1985 at 10; Leyton at 30.

71. Olsen at 119–20; Wilson and Seaman at 53–54.

72. Bockman and Taylor at 4A; Leyton at 60. See also *Murder: No Apparent Motive;* Keyes; Wilson and Seaman at 56; and Kidder.

73. Bockman and Taylor at 4A; Olsen at 159–61; "The Mind of the Mass Murderer" at 56.

74. Levin and Fox at 47; Shryock at 4.

75. Wilson and Seaman at 20–21.

76. Id. at 55; Olsen at 159–61; Wilson and Seaman at 128.

77. Egger at 266.

78. Cheney at 113, 127, 90; Bockman and Taylor at 4A.

79. Cheney at 126; *Murder: No Apparent Motive;* Keyes at 121; Wilson and Seaman at 46–49.

80. Jenkins at 10; Holmes and DeBurger (1988) at 110.

81. FBI-August 1985 at 10; Leyton at 68.

82. FBI-August at 11. The individual interviewed was not identified by the FBI research team.

83. Cheney at 147; *Murder: No Apparent Motive.*

84. Levin and Fox at 143.

85. Bockman and Taylor at 4A; Peer and Shapiro at 29.

86. Schwartz at 53, 91; O'Brien at 129; Egger at 203, 268.

87. Levin and Fox at 229–30; Lunde at 55; *Murder: No Apparent Motive;* Egger at 271–72.

88. Shryock at 4.

89. Abrahamsen (1985) at 12. This assertion was later proven false by Dr. Abrahamsen. See id. at 121.

90. O'Brien at 262–80; Egger at 263; Lacayo at 66.

91. Bartol at 55–56 (citing to Cleckley); Levin and Fox at 210.

4 Psychological Explanations

Sociopath, Psychopath, or Antisocial Personality Disorder

The most predominant psychological explanation for the serial murderer's behavior is that he suffers from an antisocial personality disorder, often referred to as psychopathy or sociopathy.[1] According to the third revised edition of the *Diagnostic and Statistical Manual of Mental Disorders* (*DSM-III-R*), an individual with such a disorder is one who displays a pattern of irresponsible and antisocial behavior; he lies, steals, initiates fights, fails to plan ahead, is irritable, reckless, unable to hold a job, and feels no remorse for the effects that his conduct has on others. The *DSM-III-R* indicates that the more flagrant of this type of behavior usually diminishes after age thirty.[2] And, in *The Mask of Sanity*, a classic examination of the psychopath, Hervey Cleckley, a noted authority on the subject, lists, among others, the following characteristics: superficial charm; intelligence; absence of delusions or irrational thinking; lack of nervousness; unreliable, untruthful, and insincere; exhibits poor judgment and fails to learn from experience; pathologic egocentricity and incapable of love; lacks specific insight; unresponsive in dealing with interpersonal relations; displays fantastic and uninviting behavior when drinking and sometimes without; sex life is impersonal, trivial, and poorly integrated; and fails to follow any specific life plan.[3]

The antisocial personality disorder, or psychopathy, is thus characterized by a wide range of behavioral patterns common among serial killers. Indeed, most of the men already mentioned have exhibited many of these traits throughout their lives. It is therefore easy to understand how a majority of psychiatrists and researchers are quick to explain serial murder as the act of a psychopath.

This rapid assessment, however, is sorely inadequate. It merely describes some of the outward characteristics apparent in the serial killer's behavior; it tells very little about how his behavior started or how it developed. Moreover, the traits of the psychopathic personality are present in people who never commit crimes of any sort. It exists in far too many nonviolent individuals to make its use beneficial in the search for what motivates the serial murderer. Recognizing the inadequacy of this broad description of psychopathy, researchers have developed a more detailed classification system, which divides psychopathic behavior into three types: primary, secondary, and dyssocial. Although individuals in each group are considered psychopaths by psychiatrists, there are important differences.

The primary psychopath is the individual who most resembles Cleckley's descriptive criteria. He is the true psychopath in that he experiences neither the psychological nor the physiological aspects of anxiety or fear. His judgment is poor, and his behavior is often guided by impulse and immediate needs. He is usually not violent or extremely destructive, although he can be at times. Rather, the primary psychopath is more likely to be involved in petty crimes such as joyriding or car theft. His criminal actions are most frequently seen as highly immature pranks performed repeatedly without regard for the embarrassment or personal risk they entail.[4]

The secondary psychopath commits antisocial or violent acts because he suffers from emotional problems or inner conflicts. On the surface, he appears to be psychopathic because of his repeated criminal behavior. Upon closer examination, however, it is usually found that he is struggling with an intense fear or anxiety from within at the time of the crime. Because of this underlying inner conflict, he is sometimes also referred to as an acting-out neurotic, neurotic delinquent, symptomatic psychopath, or neurotic character.[5]

Including this type of individual in a classification of psychopaths is misleading, since the motivation behind his acts, as well as his personality structure, life history, and response to treatment are usually very different from the true psychopath. Moreover, unlike the true psychopath, this person is capable of experiencing guilt and remorse and is able to form meaningful, affectional relationships.[6] He exhibits varied emotions and, in fact, is motivated to commit his crimes specifically because of his inner turmoil. Thus, the secondary psychopath is not actually a psychopath in the real sense of the term. Nevertheless, since his repeated criminal acts appear to be psychopathic in nature, he is labeled a secondary psychopath.

The dyssocial psychopath demonstrates aggressive, antisocial behavior because he grew up in a delinquent subculture or in an environment that fostered and rewarded such behavior. His actions, although considered deviant by society, conform to the norms of his own group of friends, gang, or family. Unlike the true psychopath, this individual is capable of strong loyalties and close relationships with those of his own group, which, together with secondary psychopaths, represents a large segment of the entire criminal population.[7]

When classifying the serial murderer as a psychopath, it is obvious that he does not fit well into the category of the primary or true psychopath. First, as previously discussed, the serial killer experiences mounting tension and anxiety before he murders, and these emotions are absent in the primary psychopath. Second, the latter's extreme tendency toward impulsive behavior, and his lack of any long-term purpose in life, prevents him from performing any criminal activity in a consistent, professional manner.[8] Third, he is unable to tolerate routine and becomes quickly bored. Finally, the primary psychopath is more likely to participate in hastily planned actions for immediate gratification.[9]

In stark contrast to the primary psychopath's behavior, the serial killer is methodic and "professional" in carrying out his murderous crimes. Although his first attempts may be unsuccessful, he quickly becomes a skilled practitioner of his "craft." Moreover, he displays a definite pattern or regularity, which is not present in the primary psychopath.[10] Likewise, the serial killer behaves differently while in confinement. Kemper's work habits, for instance, puzzled doctors at the Atascadero State Hospital, where he had been institutionalized as a teenager. In the psychology laboratory, Kemper tested patients and eventually served as a crew leader. In fact, one psychiatrist recalled that he was a very good worker, noting that this is not typical of a primary psychopath, the category into which he had been placed.[11]

Gacy also continues to flourish as a model prisoner while in confinement. Since the primary psychopath is unable to tolerate routine, this behavior distinguishes him from the serial killer, who thrives in the habitual life of a confined setting. And he is clearly not within the dyssocial psychopath group either. Although the serial murderer may act with an accomplice, there is no evidence that he participates in gang rivalry or in any type of group behavior that promotes antisocial conduct. On the contrary, he generally remains a loner throughout his life and in his crimes.

Of the three categories, the serial killer most closely resembles the secondary psychopath. Like this individual, the former also engages in repeated criminal acts. In addition, just as with the secondary psychopath, the serial killer experiences a mounting anxiety and tension that intensifies between each murder. However, there are significant differences. Unlike the secondary psychopath, the serial killer does not experience guilt or remorse as a result of his crimes. Moreover, he is unable to form close, affectional relationships with others, although he may mimic appropriate behavior when dealing with friends, lovers, and acquaintances.

Despite these differences, both types of individuals share one important common characteristic. Although the primary psychopath may function normally in all other respects, he exhibits little or no emotion. Because of this dissociation of emotion, crucial elements of normal human experience are never integrated into the psychopath's personality. Particularly, strong affective components that ordinarily arise in personal and social relationships are eliminated or blocked by this dissociation.[12] The result is an inability to feel love, anxiety, or remorse. Similarly, the serial murderer is unable to relate to the pain and suffering he inflicts upon his victims. Somehow he is incapable of any normal emotions. He can fabricate seemingly appropriate behavior, but he fails to understand the gravity of his actions. Thus, although the serial killer, like the primary psychopath, can outwardly simulate acceptable human responses, his living (in a subjective sense) is mechanical and machinelike because the essential emotional components of his psychological makeup are not present.[13] This makes it easy for the serial killer to murder, since for him the crime is emotionless and means nothing.

To replace these missing emotions, the serial murderer, like the primary psychopath, develops a system of responses to stimuli which is more a reaction of reflex than of feeling. In this way, he presents a facade of normalcy to the public, yet he is psychologically incapable of truly understanding that which he mimics. Unlike the primary psychopath, however, this inability to experience basic human emotions seems to coexist with the intense anxiety and tension felt by the serial killer immediately before he commits a murder. Therefore, he is not completely devoid of all feelings; it is only the emotions associated with empathy for others that he lacks.

Thus the serial killer's behavior, like that of the primary psychopath, may be due in part to a deficient psychological makeup that prevents normal emotional development. Relying upon this factor to explain serial murder, however, is insufficient since the cause of this deficiency in psychopaths is complex and not well understood. Indeed, many researchers claim that psychopathic behavior, like many other human illnesses, can result from a number of causes and is affected by personality, the environment, and individual life experiences.[14] Accordingly, they conclude that it is the combination of biological, sociological, and psychological factors working together that culminates in psychopathic behavior.

As we shall see in the following chapters, this theory as to the "cause" of psychopathy may be true, but it poses a serious problem for psychologists who attempt to explain that the serial murderer kills because he is a psychopath. As already pointed out, this assertion does nothing more than describe the outward characteristics displayed by the serial murderer; it does not show how an individual becomes a serial murderer since it fails to state precisely how psychopathy develops. Furthermore, it merely postulates that several factors from many areas of life contribute to psychopathic behavior. Such a general diagnosis does little in the search for what motivates this type of killer.

More importantly, however, it is clear that serial murder does not occur simply as a result of psychopathy. The categories of primary, secondary, and dyssocial psychopath encompass a wide range of individuals, including both criminal and noncriminal members of society. Since the overwhelming majority of these people exist without resorting to serial murder, something more, in addition to any psychopathic tendencies, must be at work within the serial killer to motivate his criminal acts. Explaining serial murder as the result of psychopathy thus leaves an incomplete description of what actually prompts its occurrence.

Bundy, in somewhat of a self-analysis, indicated that the psychopathy experienced by the serial killer is unlike any of the traditional forms discussed above. He described the psychopathy of the serial murderer as more of a hybrid variety, explaining that an "entity" exists within the killer and nurtures itself upon thoughts of sexual violence and pornography. These thoughts shape and direct the entity, with the illness inside the killer drawing him toward ever-increasing displays of violence. This hybrid form of psychopathy is one in which the entity is both in and of the killer, not some alien presence but a purely destructive power that grows from within.[15]

This characterization of the serial murderer as a hybrid form of psychopath appears to be fairly accurate, according to some researchers.[16] Although he possesses many qualities of both the primary and secondary psychopath, the serial killer does not fit squarely within either group; rather, he seems to be a combination of the two. Nevertheless, even if accurate, this hybrid explanation leaves open several important questions. For example, how does this psychopathic entity originate within the killer? Nor does it tell us how his violent behavior begins or why his acts become more and more violent.

Assuming that the serial murderer is some form of hybrid psychopath, the question still remains: Why does he turn to murder while the majority of psychopaths do not? Part of the answer may lie in the work of Herbert Quay, who maintains that an important characteristic underlying Cleckley's description of the psychopath is his "profound and pathological stimulation-seeking activity." Pointing out that many psychopaths are drawn to such interests as race car driving, skydiving, and motorcycle stunts, Quay asserts that their actions are motivated by an excessive physiological need for thrills and excitement.[17]

Furthermore, Quay postulates that this heightened need for stimulation is attributable either to a lowering of the brain's ability to react to sensory input or to a rapid adaptation to stimuli within the brain. In either case, the result is an increased desire for

excitement.[18] Thus, he bases his theory strongly upon the physiological processes within the body. We shall see in Chapter 6 that
researchers in the biological field have identified several areas of
the brain that may be directly related to Quay's theory of
stimulation-seeking behavior. The possibility that this type of
process has an influence on the psychological motivation of serial
murder, however, warrants further discussion.

Such a theory seems plausible; indeed, the same type of
behavior is readily seen and understood in most people on a
regular basis. Through common experience, it is known that we
try to avoid becoming trapped in the routine of daily life. Although this is almost inevitable, every person seeks variety from
time to time in order to maintain adequate levels of arousal as
well as emotional well-being. If new experiences are never sought,
boredom, irritability, and emotional depression can set in. To
prevent these adverse effects, individuals look for new stimulation
by changing jobs, taking a vacation, or simply going for a drive
in an unfamiliar area. In this way, they are engaging in stimulation-seeking behavior. The level of the activity pursued at any
given time will depend upon the amount of stimulation necessary to satisfy their needs.

If the psychopath, because of some deficiency (whether it be
biological, sociological, or psychological), requires higher levels
of activity to maintain an adequate state of arousal, this helps to
explain why he enjoys risky, exciting sports, such as skydiving or
race car driving, which offer more stimuli than those found in a
conventional life-style. Furthermore, it is easy to see why some
psychopaths turn to crime. Only through illegal acts are they able
to obtain the stimuli needed to maintain a heightened level of
arousal. Indeed, if this is true, it also accounts for the psychopath's
reluctance to stop his illegal activity even when he is caught
repeatedly. If the serial murderer is a hybrid form of psychopath,
it is possible that he possesses an even greater need for increased
stimuli than that required by the psychopath. If so, the serial
killer is therefore not satisfied with minor crimes but must resort
to the brutal act of murder in order to satisfy his heightened need
for stimulation. This, in combination with his inability to feel any
emotion for his victims, explains why the serial killer engages in
his murderous activity again and again.

This explanation, however, is speculation at this point, since no data are available to prove it conclusively. It assumes many facts that have not been satisfactorily shown, not the least of which is that the serial murderer is actually some form of psychopath. Moreover, even if he is a psychopath, there is no evidence that even hints at the notion that the serial killer has an increased need for stimulation over and above that of the psychopath. Thus this theory, while possible, has not been empirically supported. In addition, as with other psychopathic-based theories, it does not explain what initially prompts the serial killer to turn to murder for his stimulation as opposed to some other nonviolent or noncriminal activity. Accordingly, the answer to this, and to many other questions, remains unresolved.

Although the serial murderer bears a striking resemblance to the psychopath, it is obvious that there are marked differences between these two types of individuals. When psychiatrists, law enforcement authorities, or researchers simply indicate that the serial murderer kills because he is a psychopath, they fail to recognize these important differences. Moreover, by relying on this theory, they neglect to explain how an individual develops into or becomes a serial murderer. The result is an incomplete conclusory statement regarding the motivation behind serial murder.

Sexual Sadism

Dr. Donald Lunde, in *Murder and Madness*, proposes another theory, asserting that mass murderers, in general, are almost always insane. He classifies them into two groups: paranoid schizophrenics and sexual sadists. In discussing the first category, Lunde describes paranoid schizophrenia as a psychosis characterized by hallucinations, delusions, bizarre religious ideas, suspicion, and aggression.[19] There is no evidence that the serial killer possesses any of these symptoms. As already seen, he shows no signs of mental illness; thus, this classification does not fit the serial killer.

It must be recognized, however, that there are those individuals who do kill repeatedly over a period of time as a result of psychotic delusions or hallucinations. For example, Joseph

Kallinger, who murdered three people, including his own son, between July 1974 and January 1975, suffered from paranoid schizophrenia. He claimed that the voice of the Lord told him to kill three billion people, after which he would become a god. He also was prompted by a hallucination called Charlie, the floating head of a young boy that taunted him into committing murder.[20] Clearly, the motivating force here is the killer's psychotic break with reality. This type of murderer is quite obviously different from the serial murderer and does not fit the profile established in Chapter 3. Although he may kill numerous people one at a time over a long period, he is not the serial murderer who is the subject of this book.

Lunde's second classification, the sexual sadist, seems to describe the serial killer more appropriately. In fact, Lunde uses Edmund Kemper as an example, arguing that he suffered from sexual sadism, a condition characterized by torturing, killing, and mutilating persons in order to achieve sexual gratification.[21] Rather than merely delighting in cruelty, it is a perversion in which sexual gratification is obtained through the infliction of pain and degradation of others. The sexual sadist murders because, for him, the act of killing and abusing his victims produces a powerful sexual arousal. Indeed, the violent attack often seems to serve as a substitute for actual sexual intercourse.[22]

If the serial killer is a sexual sadist, his crimes thus serve to stimulate sexual arousal and afford him gratification that cannot otherwise be achieved. This notion may have some validity, since in some instances the murders are accompanied by ejaculation, sexual assaults, or some form of sexual deviance. Leyton argues, however, that, although the serial killer's sexuality may be part of the reason for the attack, it is more of an afterthought than a motivating force. In comparing DeSalvo, Kemper, Bundy, and Berkowitz, he maintains that any sexual release that was present was not a prime motive; rather, it was simply an extra benefit of the task at hand.[23] Nevertheless, although this sadistic behavior cannot be attributed to all serial killers, a further exploration into the cause of sexual sadism is warranted.

In describing how an individual becomes a sexual sadist, Lunde explains that, for some unknown reason, sexual and violent impulses merge in childhood. Once this merger starts, it may progress to such an extent that these impulses become inextricably interwoven. When this occurs the individual feels compelled to perform a brutal, violent act in order to achieve sexual satisfaction. Dr. David Abrahamsen concurs that the emotions of love and hate are closely intertwined, expounding that the sexual drive in humans is also intimately associated with hateful and murderous thoughts and actions.[24]

Although this hypothesis that sexually sadistic behavior results from the merger of sexual and violent impulses may be true, it brings us no closer to discovering why the serial murderer repeatedly kills. No explanation is given as to why these impulses combine. Moreover, many individuals often display extreme sadistic behavior without ever becoming serial murderers; indeed, many never kill. In addition, it is well recognized that sadism is not confined to any one type of personality, since it occurs in people from all walks of life. Even sadistic murderers are quite different from one another, their only common trait many times being their need to exercise cruelty and power over others.[25] Thus, simply explaining serial murder as the result of a sexual sadist's actions provides no real clue into the psychiatric motivation for this type of crime. For this theory to be of any use, then, it is necessary to probe further into the reasons for such violent behavior.

Manfred Guttmacher, a psychiatrist, has postulated that pure sadistic murderers are nearly always psychotic and that many of them are sexually impotent.[26] If serial killers are sexual sadists, this theory explains why they experience difficulty in normal sexual or intimate relationships with their wives or girlfriends. However, as already seen, they are not psychotic in the traditional sense, since they do not suffer from the hallucinations or delusions commonly associated with psychotic disorders.

It is important to distinguish, however, between two different definitions of the word psychotic. The first describes the traditional, clinical term whereby the individual suffers from hallucinations or delusions. The second, used by Hans Eysenck, describes a disorder similar to that seen in the primary psychopath. According to Eysenck, psychotic behavior is characterized by cold-blooded cruelty, insensitivity, lack of emotion, disregard for danger, troublesome behavior, and hostility toward others.[27] In this sense, serial killers may exhibit psychotic tendencies since they display many of these traits. From our earlier discussion, however, it is clear that serial killers do not fall squarely within the primary psychopath category. Since Eysenck's psychotics do, it is uncertain whether serial murderers can be classified as such even in this sense of the word. Moreover, with either definition, it cannot be said that they are nearly always psychotic.

In a further explanation of what causes sexually sadistic behavior, Benjamin Karpman, a noted psychiatrist at St. Elizabeth's Hospital in Washington, DC, postulates that the exciting stimuli involved in the act of murder affect the nervous pathways of that part of the brain associated with erection and ejaculation.[28] As will be seen in Chapter 6, this thinking finds some support in biological research. It also comports with the psychological theory of the merger of sexual and aggressive impulses in the psyche. As applied to the serial murderer, however, no research has been done in this area, and it thus remains speculation.

Still another theory on sadistic behavior proposes that the sexual sadist tortures his victim until, because of the intensity of the suffering, the victim is forced to "forgive" his assailant. According to this reasoning, the killer's pleasure and sexual satisfaction are blocked by his feelings of guilt about his behavior. He continues his torture until he makes the victim forgive his acts, thereby releasing the murderer's guilt and thus allowing him to experience sexual gratification.[29] The amount of pain inflicted is therefore dependent upon how long it takes for the victim's forgiveness. If it is not forthcoming, the violence continues and the victim is eventually killed.

This theory, however, does not seem to apply to serial killers such as Bundy and Gacy. Since most of Bundy's victims were rendered unconscious by a blow to the head before they were killed, they obviously could not have been forced to forgive their attacker. And, although many of the young men were conscious prior to their deaths, there is no evidence that Gacy sought their forgiveness before killing them. Thus, the validity of this theory, as it applies to the serial killer, is doubtful.

Other researchers attempting to discover how a sadistic murderer develops look to his childhood for answers. They find that these individuals usually were raised by brutal and abusive parents, with whom they formed a close identification and from whom they learned that violence is a solution to frustration.[30] This pattern also applies to the serial killer, since he, too, often grows up in an unhealthy, violent, and even dangerous environment. His early experiences may very well be the foundation for his sadistic behavior later in life.

Lunde has pointed out one important characteristic of the sexual sadist that seems to apply equally to the serial killer: the dehumanization of his victims. He explains that a sex murderer sees his victims not as human beings but as life-size dolls, thereby making the act of murder easier since it prevents him from identifying with his victims as people.[31] Similarly, the serial killer does not want to know his victims personally and usually avoids even learning their names or anything about their lives. Rather, he wishes to view them as nonentities or inanimate objects. In this way, the mental posture of the serial killer closely resembles that of the sexual sadist.

The sadistic murderer, as described above, also has been called a lust murderer. It is the contention of some, however, that this type of individual is unique and is distinguished from the sadistic murderer because he often mutilates his victim's breasts, rectum, or genitals.[32] Nevertheless, because the lust murderer exhibits the same type of brutal behavior as the sadistic killer, a discussion of him is warranted at this point.

The classification of the lust murderer is composed of two types of killer: the organized nonsocial and the disorganized asocial. The former often grows up in a home where parental discipline was inconsistent. As an adult, he exhibits a complete indifference to the interests and welfare of society and is irresponsible and self-centered. Although he dislikes people generally, he is able to display an amiable facade in order to manipulate them. He is methodic and cunning, usually possessing an average or above average IQ, and he is fully cognizant of the wrongfulness of his acts as well as their impact on society. Stress, such as problems with finances, marriage, or employment, often precedes the attack. Generally, he lives some distance from the crime scene and will cruise for a victim. While committing the murder, he is usually calm and relaxed, and alcohol is occasionally consumed prior to the act. At the time of his crime, he is most often living with a partner or spouse, with whom he is sexually competent.[33]

In contrast is the asocial lust murderer, who usually has experienced harsh and even brutal parental discipline as a child. By the time he is grown, he has developed an extreme aversion to society and isolates himself from others, preferring his own company. He has difficulty with interpersonal relationships and is sexually incompetent, often never achieving any level of sexual intimacy. He perceives that he is constantly being rejected, and is often quite lonely. He has a pattern of inconsistent or poor work history and acts impulsively under stress. Furthermore, he lacks the cleverness of the nonsocial type, normally having a below average IQ. His crimes are likely to be committed in close proximity to his home or place of business, where he feels more secure, and are usually committed in a frenzied, hastily planned manner.[34]

Thus, there are two distinct classifications of the lust murderer, with very different characteristics. As applied to the serial killer, this attempt to distinguish between the two types is somewhat misleading. Upon examination, it is clear that many serial killers exhibit some traits of both the nonsocial and the asocial lust murderer. Although amiable and completely comfortable in groups (nonsocial), the serial killer is also usually seen as a loner (asocial). Gacy and Berkowitz lived close to their crime scenes (asocial), but they both cruised incessantly for their victims (nonsocial). Despite his extremely manipulative behavior (nonsocial), the serial murderer also suffers from feelings of rejection and loneliness (asocial). Therefore, if the serial killer is a lust murderer, the distinction between nonsocial and asocial types cannot be drawn, since he exhibits the characteristics of both.

Critics of the lust murderer classifications point out these difficulties and argue that there is little empirical data to validate the separate categories. Indeed, many assert that the organized and disorganized offender groups are never mutually exclusive, a fact recognized by the proponents of this theory who readily admit that the two lust murderer designations are not absolute. As a result, a third category has been created termed *mixed type*, into which individuals who exhibit characteristics of both groups can be placed.[35]

Although this classification solves the problem of how to label individual serial murderers, it does not further define or identify the motivating force behind the crime. On the contrary, it broadens the realm of possible motivating forces that may be behind the killer's acts, since those in the mixed type category encompass a wide range of individuals. Moreover, it does not address the psychiatric reason for the murders; it merely describes the outward appearance of the killer. As a result, the usefulness of this theory in explaining the cause of serial murder is limited.

There is, however, one very significant characteristic that is shared by both serial and lust murderers. As already seen, fantasy plays an important role in the crimes of the serial killer. Robert Hazelwood and John Douglas, FBI special agents of the Behavioral Sciences Unit, explain that it also is a necessary part of the lust murderer's actions. They relate that, with the latter, the actual attack is precisely planned out in the obsessive fantasies of the killer, who does not consciously decide to act out his fantasies until the moment of the crime. Like those experienced by the serial murderer, these fantasies provide the lust murderer with an avenue of escape from his real world existence.[36]

Quoting Dr. James Reinhardt, Hazelwood and Douglas further explain that sadistic fantasies precede the brutal act of a lust murderer. Relying on pornographic literature and pictures to create his fantasies, the killer then dwells upon them. At some point he loses contact with reality and finds himself impelled to carry his fantasies into the real world by including his victims.[37] In this way, the imaginary life of the lust murderer eventually overpowers him and dictates his crimes. As discussed in Chapter 3, the serial killer also is consumed by his mental images of violence and aggression. What originally had provided a release for him eventually becomes a trap, thereby causing him to act out his fantasies of brutal murder.

Recognizing this phenomenon, some researchers believe that lust and serial murderers, because of some internal deficiency, cannot resist, like most of society, acting out their fantasies. Walter Bromberg, psychiatrist and professor of legal medicine, maintains that the only major difference between the average, law-abiding citizen and these types of murderers is that the former is merely a dreamer who confines himself to his fantasies, while the latter act them out. Furthermore, Bromberg believes that murderous impulses and sadistic fantasies reside in all individuals, consciously or unconsciously, but that these murderers act them out because of weak egos and inadequate repressive mechanisms. In other words, they do not possess sufficient ego control to prevent the emergence of destructive and violent impulses drawn from their fantasies. Other researchers in psychology generally agree that the serial killer commits his crimes merely because he is incapable of resisting the sadistic fantasies that are entertained, but resisted, by others.[38]

If this theory is accurate, it poses a frightening possibility: If all individuals in society harbor the sadistic, violent fantasies of the serial murderer, then everyone is a potential serial killer, and many more should emerge from society. However, while many people may fantasize about aggression, it is highly unlikely that they do so to the same extent as the serial killer. Although this theory of weak ego control seems doubtful, we shall see in Chapter 7 how it was accepted in the psychiatric field for many years. As such, it obscured the pursuit of an answer to serial murder because it led researchers away from considering other important factors that contribute to committing such a crime.

It is therefore clear that in some respects the serial murderer is very similar to the sexual sadist. The intensity of the attack and the violent fantasies preceding each crime are characteristic of both types of murder. Yet, with many serial killers, sexual impulses do not seem to be a motivating force. Accordingly, it cannot be said with any degree of certainty that serial murder is caused by sexual sadism. Although many serial killers also may be sexual sadists, this theory cannot fully account for the overall occurrence of serial murder. Other factors must be at work within the killer to motivate his acts.

Necrophilism

Because of the emphasis that some researchers place on sexual gratification as the basis for the serial killer's acts, many label him as a necrophiliac, or someone who exhibits a morbid interest in or sexually violates dead bodies.[39] Lucas readily admits to being a necrophiliac, and Gacy as well exhibited these tendencies. Jack Levin and James Fox explain that necrophilism is tied to the killer's inferiority complex. He prefers intercourse with corpses not only because it gives him a sense of mastery over the sexual encounter, but also it makes him feel secure to know that a dead sex partner is not aware of his sexual inadequacies nor can comment on his interpersonal failures. Intercourse becomes more attractive to the necrophiliac because the corpse is always there when he wants it; makes no demands; is never unfaithful, frustrating, or reproachful; and is not critical of his sexual incompetencies.[40] Kemper, for instance, has supported this theory, explaining that he felt very inadequate in social and sexual encounters and thus began to fantasize about making love to people. Soon this became dissatisfying to him, since in reality he could never carry out his role in these fantasies. Realizing his inadequacies, yet wanting to fulfill his fantasy, he knew that he would not fail if his sexual partners were dead and could not reject him as a lover.[41]

The concept of necrophilism, however, cannot fully account for serial murder. Although most serial killers suffer from feelings of inferiority, prompted in part by a failure at interpersonal relationships, it is doubtful that their crimes are motivated solely by necrophilism, since many of them sexually assault their victims before killing them. Moreover, others avoid any type of intercourse with their victims. Thus, to assert that serial murder is the result of necrophilism is erroneous, for although some individual serial killers may exhibit necrophile tendencies, this does not provide an adequate explanation of their motives.

Hatred

Another popular theory that attempts to explain why the serial killer repeatedly murders proposes that he harbors a deep animosity toward all women due to an underlying hatred for some significant female in his life, such as his mother, sister, or girlfriend. Ann Rule believed that Bundy killed women because of his failed relationship with Stephanie Brooks, using as support the fact that most of his victims closely resembled her in age and appearance. As seen in Chapter 1, after the initial crushing rejection by Stephanie, Bundy transformed himself into a man whom she would desire and then pursued her. When he finally won her heart, he abruptly called off the relationship, apparently in an attempt to hurt her as much as she had wounded him. If this rejection of Stephanie by Bundy had failed to satisfy his underlying need for revenge, or to extinguish his anger for what she had done, he may have sought to quell that rage by destroying Stephanie through the murder of young girls who looked like her.

Likewise, Kemper claims that he was driven to kill women because of the psychological abuse he had suffered at the hands of his mother. The young ladies he murdered were all students attending the college where his mother was employed, and, although they were not direct substitutes for her, they served as pseudosubstitutes. As Kemper admits, they all represented what his mother coveted and what was important to her, and through his acts he was destroying those values. When he finally killed his mother, he relates that the event was almost a catharsis. Similarly, Lucas frequently speaks of being driven by a hatred for the way his mother had raised him.[42]

In Berkowitz's case, Abrahamsen explains that there were five women in his life whom he grew to despise. The first was his stepmother, who, by marrying David's father, separated the two, leaving the boy alone. The second was his stepmother's daughter, who always seemed to upstage David. Next was his adoptive mother, whom he hated because she had died when he was fourteen, thereby "abandoning" him. The fourth was his biological mother, who gave birth to him illegitimately and then gave him up for adoption. And finally there was his half-sister, whom his own mother had kept while David had been "thrown away." While in his early twenties, Berkowitz sought out both of these women, and Abrahamsen believes that this fateful encounter may have been the precipitating event that activated his murderous impulses.[43] Although his half-sister and his real mother were cordial toward David, they did not welcome him as a close member of their family. Rather than placate his sense of alienation, they served to reinforce his feelings of worthlessness. Indeed, his first killing came just six months later.

The notion that the serial killer has formed a hatred for someone or something, and displays that enmity by murdering those who represent the detested person or object, is an example of displaced aggression. The victims are not attacked because of who they are but because they represent what the killer despises. He takes out his animosity on these individuals rather than on the person or object actually hated.[44] A common form of displaced aggression is one in which an individual has a difficult day at work and then yells at his children when he gets home. He is not angry at them but at someone or something at his job. He has displaced his anger, however, onto his children and takes it out on them.

Dr. Richard Ratner, a psychiatrist who studies serial murder, explains how this hatred in the serial killer becomes displaced upon his victims. He argues that the serial murderer may harbor a deep hatred of, or resentment for, a parent, yet at the same time be very dependent on that person. Thus, he finds himself in a frustrating situation, since he must vent these feelings but cannot chance rejection by the parent in a direct confrontation. Therefore, the anger and hate are displaced and the killer's aggressive behavior is inflicted upon a substitute figure.[45] This applies equally to the previous example of the individual who is angered at work. He cannot lose his temper with his superiors because to do so would jeopardize his job security, upon which he is dependent. Therefore, he vents his anger on a substitute figure, in this case his children. It is thus easy to see how the serial killer's hatred for someone can be displaced if he is dependent upon that person physically, emotionally, or psychologically.

It is somewhat misleading, however, to say that serial killers commit their crimes because of a hatred of women. Gacy, for instance, who murdered young men, showed no signs of disliking women, nor did Corll, Henley, and Brooks. Rather, it is more appropriate to conclude that the murders are motivated by some hatred that the killer sustains within himself. Depending upon the cause of that enmity, his anger will center on a particular type of person. In the case of Bundy, Kemper, and Berkowitz, the hatred focused on women; with Gacy, Henley, Brooks, and Corll, it was on young men and boys. Thus, the hatred within the serial killer may play an important role in the motivation of his crimes, but how it is developed and becomes focused is best answered by examining the influence of sociological and environmental factors upon the killer as he is growing up. We shall see in Chapter 5 exactly what these factors are.

Impaired Emotional Development

Several researchers studying the serial murderer suggest that his crimes stem from some form of retarded or impaired emotional development that begins in early childhood.[46] Although he physically grows to adulthood, the serial killer never seems to mature emotionally. For example, many investigators believed that Bundy was only a precocious twelve-year-old, and Berkowitz was described as a revengeful and omnipotent child.[47] Indeed, the serial murderer's actions in every aspect of his life seem to indicate an emotional immaturity and an inability to cope with difficulties. His constant lying and manipulative behavior suggest a spoiled child who continually seeks to have things his own way. In addition, his failure to maintain close, interpersonal relationships is indicative of his low level of emotional maturity, which some believe can also result in a defective, preadolescent mind that controls the actions of an adult body.[48] Since it is this younger mind that must contend with the violent and sadistic fantasies experienced by the killer, it is easy to see how the serial murderer might deal with these fantasies by acting them out in inappropriate ways.

In an attempt to explain how this emotional retardation occurs, Abrahamsen has focused on what Sigmund Freud referred to as the oral and anal stages of development. If an infant is either too frustrated or overindulged in the first year of its life (oral stage), some part of him will remain in this stage. As a result, Abrahamsen believes that he will become dependent, helpless, generous, kind, ambitious, self-righteous, cooperative, passive, calculating, unruly, and will need to be the center of attention. Between the ages of one and two and one-half years old (anal stage), a child must learn self-control. An individual who retains anal traits appears submissive and cooperative but is also manipulative and controlling, impatient, rigid, perfectionistic, and cruel.[49] While some degree of all of these characteristics is necessary for healthy development, in their extreme they can create a personality that is highly destructive. If a child does not learn proper behavior in either the oral or anal stage, his psychological development and emotional maturation beyond these stages can be disrupted, thereby preventing him from reaching emotional maturity.

According to this highly psychoanalytic theory, then, the serial killer is the product of an impaired emotional development caused by improper parenting. Because of this deficiency, he also may be the result of an inability to adapt psychologically to the increasing expectations and frustrations placed upon him during childhood. Consequently, this emotional retardation renders him ill prepared to deal with adult responsibilities. Both of these ideas are very similar to the theories on how the psychopath develops and were explored earlier in this chapter.

However, a theory espousing impaired emotional growth leads to the conclusion that the serial killer's behavior is already formed by the age of three, thereby seemingly discounting what he learns later in life. As we shall discover in Chapter 5, experiences occurring throughout childhood, adolescence, and early adulthood may have dramatic effects upon the serial killer as well. It is therefore a mistake to rely solely upon these psychoanalytic theories of development in attempting to explain serial murder.

Although these theories certainly may be contributing factors, they are not the driving force behind the serial murderer's acts of violence. In discussing the development of Berkowitz, for instance, Abrahamsen claims that David was irreparably harmed by discovering at an early age that he was adopted, explaining that, if children are told of their adoption too early, it can lead to an individual who is shameful, anxious, confused, distrustful, shows hate and rage, establishes poor family relationships, and retreats into an intense fantasy life.[50] He then points to this as support for an explanation of Berkowitz's improper emotional development, based on the separation-individuation theory.

According to Abrahamsen, during the first three years of life, a child is entirely dependent upon its mother for survival. Along with this dependency, however, the child must fully establish its own individuality, separate and apart from its mother, by the age of two and one-half to three years old. During this critical period of development, Abrahamsen believes that Berkowitz somehow sensed that he was adopted, and this knowledge kept him from relying upon his mother for support while developing his individuality. As a result, the natural process of separation between David and his mother was never fully completed, thereby preventing an alliance between the two and causing an inability, on

Berkowitz's part, to accept either of his parents. He therefore was more vulnerable to emotional problems normally encountered in life.[51] Thus, Abrahamsen again uses a psychoanalytic or Freudian theory to explain the behavior of the serial murderer.

The difficulty with the above theories is that it is almost impossible to prove or disprove their premises and conclusions. The concepts do not easily lend themselves to clinical testing or evaluation by objective standards. They are more subjective discussions based upon one psychological school of thought that tends to discount other ideas as well as different fields of study, such as sociology or biology. Apart from this, the purely psychoanalytical theories postulated do not, by themselves, adequately explain why the serial murderer repeatedly kills. Many individuals exhibit characteristics of the oral and anal stage of development, and numerous adopted children suffer emotional trauma as a result of their adoption, yet they do not become serial killers. Even if these theories do describe how some serial murderers develop, something more must be involved to produce this methodic killer.

In spite of these criticisms, the retardation of emotional development appears to be an accepted theory among many psychologists to explain the serial killer's motivation. However, to complement this psychological explanation as well as others already mentioned, it is essential that additional factors affecting human behavior in general, and the serial killer in particular, also be discussed. Thus, we now turn to the sociological explanations of serial murder.

Notes

1. This disorder has been designated by various labels. In 1800 it was termed *manie sans délire* (mania without delirium). In 1872 individuals suffering with this disorder were considered "morally insane," and the term *psychopath* was adopted at that time. In 1952 the American Psychiatric Association substituted the word *sociopath*, and in 1972 the World Health Organization introduced the term *antisocial personality*. Despite these changes in terminology the disorder's characteristics have generally remained the same. See *Encyclopedia of Crime and Justice* at 1315.

2. *Diagnostic and Statistical Manual of Mental Disorders* (3d rev. ed.) at 342 (hereafter *DSM-III-R*).

3. Cleckley at 337–38.

4. Hare at 6; Bartol at 53–54.

5. Hare at 7; Karpman at 113; Wilson and Herrnstein at 206; Bartol at 54–55.

6. Hare at 8.

7. Id.; Bartol at 54–55.

8. Quay at 180; Wilson and Herrnstein at 204–5; Bartol at 57.

9. Quay at 180; Bartol at 58.

10. Cleckley at 343.

11. Cheney at 30, 201; Leyton at 64.

12. Cleckley at 371, 374.

13. Id. at 383.

14. Craft at 26; Bartol at 61.

15. Throughout the interviews described in Michaud and Aynesworth, Bundy spoke in the third person, never admitting personal responsibility for the crimes committed. He provided not only detailed accounts of how the victims were killed but also an explanation of "the killer's" motives. Most psychiatrists agree that he was actually describing his own crimes and motivations, although speaking in the third person and using "hypotheticals." See Michaud and Aynesworth at 21–22.

16. Cartel at x.

17. Quay at 180–83. See also Bartol at 59; and Wilson and Herrnstein at 199.

18. Quay at 181.

19. Lunde at 48.

20. See Schreiber at 218, 209, 316–18.

21. Lunde at 53–56, 48.

22. MacDonald at 164; Lunde at 53; *DSM-III-R* at 287; Liebert at 191, 195.

23. Leyton at 135, 147. See also Egger at 227.

24. Lunde at 53, 56; Abrahamsen (1985) at 162.

25. MacDonald at 25.

26. Guttmacher at 95.

27. Bartol at 40 (citing to Hans J. Eysenck, *The Inequality of Man* [San Diego: EDITS, 1973]; "The Biology of Morality," in *Moral Development and Behavior*, ed. Thomas Lickona [New York: Holt, Rinehart and Winston, 1976, 108–23]).

28. See Guttmacher at 95 (citing to Benjamin Karpman, *The Sexual Offender and His Offenses* [New York: Julian Press, 1954]).

29. See Guttmacher at 95–96 (citing to Otto Fenichel, *The Psychoanalytic Theory of Neurosis* [New York: W. W. Norton, 1945]).

30. See Guttmacher at 96 (citing to Glen M. Duncan et al., "Etiological Factors in First Degree Murder," *Journal of American Medical Association* 168 [November 1958]: 1755–58).

31. Lunde at 61.

32. Guttmacher at 95; Hazelwood and Douglas at 18.

33. FBI-August 1985 at 19.

34. Id. at 22; Hazelwood and Douglas at 19.

35. Holmes and DeBurger (1988) at 100; Ressler et al. (1986a) at 293; Michaud at 75; Holmes and DeBurger (1988) at 53–55; FBI-August 1985 at 22.

36. Hazelwood and Douglas at 21.

37. Id. (citing to James Reinhardt, *Sex Perversions and Sex Crimes* [Springfield, IL: Charles C. Thomas, 1957]).

38. See Bartol at 219–20 (citing to Walter Bromberg, *The Mold of Murder: A Psychiatric Study of Homicide* [New York: Grune and Stratton, 1961]). See also Guttmacher at 95; and Abrahamsen (1973).
39. See *Taber's Cyclopedic Medical Dictionary* at 1187.
40. Levin and Fox at 35; MacDonald at 174 (citing to H. Segal, "A Necrophilic Phantasy," *International Journal of Psychoanalysis* 34 [1953]: 98–101).
41. Lunde at 55.
42. *Murder: No Apparent Motive*; Egger at 269.
43. Abrahamsen (1985) at 86, 72–75, 90.
44. See Shryock at 4.
45. From the film *Murder: No Apparent Motive*. See also Foreman at 18-A.
46. Abrahamsen (1985) at 108; Michaud and Aynesworth at 21; Rule at 338.
47. Michaud and Aynesworth at 21; Abrahamsen (1985) at 108.
48. Michaud and Aynesworth at 21.
49. Abrahamsen (1985) at 55–56.
50. Abrahamsen (1985) at 68 (citing to Herbert Wieder, "The Family Romance Fantasies of Adopted Children," *Psychoanalytic Quarterly* 46(2) [April 1977]: 185–200).
51. Id. at 68–69 (citing to Margaret Mahler, *On Human Symbiosis and the Vicissitudes of Individuation* [New York: International University Press, 1968]; Bernard L. Pacella and Myron S. Hurvich, "The Significance of Symbiosis and Separation-Individuation for Psychiatric Theory and Practice," in *Mental Health in Children*, ed. D. Siva Sankar [New York: PJD Publications, 1969]; David Abrahamsen, *The Emotional Care of Your Child* [New York: Trident Press, 1969]).

5 Sociological Explanations

Childhood Deprivation

Any sociological examination of what motivates human behavior must start at the beginning of life. Environmental factors are perhaps the most influential and very often have a permanent effect in shaping the later development of a child. Most researchers agree that children who are cared for and loved while growing up will be healthier, more productive, and better adjusted to deal with society. In contrast, those who are subjected to violence, neglect, or abuse will experience extreme difficulty in coping with life's demands.[1]

As already seen, the serial killer's childhood is marked by a lack of nurturing and love. He usually grows up in a neglectful, abusive, and even violent atmosphere, where important needs are not met. Indeed, many suffer from physical, sexual, or psychological mistreatment at the hands of their parents. Researchers are now finding that most children who are abused often display more aggression and frustration than other children and are much less likely to form close, personal relationships with their parents, who are less inclined to initiate any meaningful contact with them.[2] The end result is children who are not only mistreated but also very lonely.

Abused children often experience a wide range of emotional problems that are rooted in even the earliest abuse and are fueled by continued mistreatment. Eventually, they find it very difficult to deal with their own feelings, as well as with other people. They may suffer from a sense of mistrust toward self and others, an inability to establish meaningful interpersonal or sexual relationships, feelings of low self-worth, lack of basic social skills, a sense of helplessness, failure to make decisions, unplanned life goals, difficulty in expressing feelings, and an underlying anger, guilt, and depression.[3] Such problems are clearly seen in the serial murderer, who is often incapable of maintaining close relationships with anyone and suffers from low self-esteem. Like the abused child, his personality and character are such that he is completely unable to cope with the emotional demands of life.

Adults who were abused as children also tend to exhibit inexplicable violent outbursts, and, in some cases, there are no apparent precipitating events. The individual simply acts in such a manner for no reason at all, often not even feeling any corresponding anger or rage. In fact, it almost seems that the person becomes disassociated from the event. Furthermore, the abused child usually has an incessant need to be perfect. He believes that he must be the best at everything he does, an obsession that continues well into adulthood.[4] In much the same way, serial murderers exhibit these qualities. They are forever striving to be an overwhelming success in all that they do, and they often exhibit sudden violent outbursts and are unable to cope with the emotional demands of society. These similarities offer important clues as to the initial stages of the development of the serial killer.

In addition to the emotional impact suffered by abused children, their unhealthy home atmosphere is often the classroom for learning how to handle behavioral problems. It is generally accepted that children adopt many forms of behavior merely by watching and imitating their parents, a process known as modeling or observational learning.[5] If a parent reacts to stress and frustration with an aggressive or violent response, a child will learn that such behavior is an acceptable reaction, and he then will handle stressful situations accordingly as he grows. Usually his violence is expressed through mild temper tantrums or much more aggressively by fighting.

Moreover, it has been noted that children who are punished physically (external restraints) rather than psychologically— that is, for instance, by verbal shaming or by withholding love (internal restraints)—are more likely to express their aggressive feelings toward others in a physical manner and are less likely to use internal restraints.[6] Indeed, many researchers claim that physical punishment has no positive effect on the behavior of children at all. On the contrary, they believe that it adversely affects childhood behavior by making misconduct more, rather than less, likely. If this is true, then the more severe the punishment used by the parent the more aggressive the child will become.[7] He merely adopts a form of behavior that he learns from the parent: violent and aggressive acts are a way to solve problems and alleviate stress.

Hans Toch, professor of criminal justice at the State University of New York at Albany, supports this view of learned aggression in children, suggesting that a majority of violent episodes are the result of well-learned, systematic strategies of violence that certain personalities find to be effective in dealing with conflictual, interpersonal relationships.[8] He asserts that these individuals find out in childhood that violent responses are successful in obtaining various goals such as achieving self-worth or becoming well respected within one's community. Furthermore, Toch distinguishes between two methods used to express this type of behavior. With the first, the individual manipulates others with violence or the threat of it in an effort to satisfy his own personal needs. The second involves a violent reaction toward others when feeling threatened or vulnerable to manipulation.[9]

This first category of learned aggression is applicable to the serial murderer, who is extremely adept at controlling others and always expects to get his way. When he does not, he often exhibits outbursts of rage. The second method of expressing violence also fits the serial killer, since his attacks are a reaction to feelings of stress. As seen in Kemper and others we have examined, they experienced high levels of tension immediately before committing their crimes. The release of this mounting tension after the murder indicates that the violence involved provided the necessary relief.

It must be recognized, however, that not all children whose parents exhibit violent behavior become hardened criminals. In fact, a majority does not, although some may engage in other forms of crime. This may be the result of outside influences, such as relatives, friends, schoolteachers, and the media, who may provide positive role models for the child, thereby outweighing the negative factors found in the home. Consequently, an individual is less likely to resort to aggressive behavior as a means of coping. Of course, the presence of some aggressive tendencies is necessary in order to prevent the development of an overly passive individual. What is important is to strike a balance between aggressive and passive behavior and to teach the child when an aggressive response is appropriate and when it is unacceptable.

The consistency of punishment used is therefore very important. If a parent slaps his child simply because the parent is aggravated or irritated by behavior that is usually permitted and without regard to whether the child has broken a specific rule, such punishment is not likely to produce observance of the rule. On the contrary, because the discipline is random or erratic, and not clearly based upon some behavior defined by a set rule, it may lead the child to believe that violence is an acceptable method of expressing one's feelings, no matter what the provocation or the consequence might be.[10] This inconsistency not only confuses the child but also increases his use of aggressive behavior.

Researchers generally agree that most often the parents of antisocial children are less likely than others to state clear rules, demand compliance with those rules, or punish children when these are violated.[11] Rather, they ignore some transgressions while unpredictably punishing for others. The result of this inconsistent behavior is a child who only understands that violence is the way to deal with stress. He learns by example that, when he is frustrated, the best reaction is to lash out at those around him. In addition, the child feels, quite accurately, that he cannot control what happens to him by his own actions. No matter how well he behaves, he still will be punished. Consequently, he suffers from a type of stress known as learned helplessness, whereby he finds himself powerless to avoid punishment and is at the mercy of his parents' erratic shifts in mood and behavior.[12] The result is an individual who has no control over whether he is beaten or praised.

It is clear that abusive parents, or those whose discipline is harsh or inconsistent, raise children who see violence as the only means of dealing with difficulties in life. Since most serial murderers experience abusive or harsh childhoods, they also never learn when aggressiveness is appropriate and when it is not. As a response to stress, the serial killer understands only that aggressive behavior offers relief. Thus, he may resort to violence because he has learned that it is the only means of alleviating stress or coping with problems.

This theory of learned aggression therefore seems to have a great deal of validity. However, it fails to explain serial killers such as Berkowitz or Bundy, whose childhood experiences were not marked by their parents' violence or aggressive behavior. Indeed, there is no evidence at all of severe abuse. Although violent behavior learned in childhood seems to be an important part of what motivates many serial murderers, it cannot be the determinate factor.

Even without the presence of severe abuse, the existence of an inadequate homelife still may play a pivotal role in the development of the serial murderer. In the case of Berkowitz and Bundy, their home environment did not provide sufficient love and nurturing to promote a healthy development. As already seen, neither enjoyed a very close relationship with their parents. The guidance they needed was absent, and this may have had a severe impact on their formative years. Indeed, one theory suggests that parental neglect or lack of affection is a frustrating circumstance that engenders distrust of all others, prevents emotional attachments, and leads to resentful, angry, and hostile attitudes toward people in general.[13] Quite often a child exposed to this type of upbringing exhibits an initial phase of dependent behavior, followed by indiscriminate friendliness, culminating in a personality characterized by a lack of guilt and an inability to obey rules or form lasting relationships. In addition, the child suffers from a weak ego, low self-esteem, impulsiveness, and aggressiveness.[14]

Thus, the establishment of emotional ties in childhood is vitally important. If no attachments between parent and child are formed, the development of the child can be severely impaired. Indeed, children who are deprived of a nurturing homelife suffer from many of the same emotional problems as do abused children, thereby suggesting that it is not merely the presence of violence in the home but rather the lack of love and proper nurturing that prompts aggressive behavior. This theory has gained wide support among researchers.[15] It not only explains the genesis of aggressive behavior in general but also the development of the psychopath,[16] in which two kinds of parental behaviors are described as contributing factors. In the first type, the parents are cold and distant, allowing no close relationships to develop between them and the child. With the second, discipline, rewards, and punishment are inconsistent and capricious. Instead of learning right from wrong, the child discovers how to avoid blame and punishment by lying or by other manipulative means.[17] Therefore, this explanation lends support to the theory that the later aggressive behavior of the psychopath, as well as the serial killer, is learned.

Furthermore, it is postulated that emotional deprivation or rejection by parents, together with other environmental factors or damage to inhibitive centers of the brain, best accounts for the development of the psychopath.[18] However, Cleckley argues that too much emphasis is placed on the notion of parental rejection, stating that, if there is any negative element in a family's background contributing to the behavior of the psychopath, it is extremely subtle. He concedes, though, that an adverse effect on the child's development could result if the parent has an incapacity to express warmth and affection. Although the parent may be fair, kind, and demonstrate other admirable qualities, he or she may lack that one essential ingredient necessary to form a close relationship with the child.[19] Unfortunately, Cleckley does not indicate what this one vital element is. Nevertheless, he does recognize that some sociological factors play a part in the formation of antisocial and aggressive behavior.

A final theory that relates parental behavior to the development of the psychopath postulates that such an individual is the result of pampering and overindulgence, which allows the child to escape punishment for his antisocial and aggressive behavior. By merely apologizing and promising not to misbehave, the child learns to manipulate others and thereby avoids responsibility for his psychopathic actions. The parents' failure to enforce discipline reinforces his antisocial attitudes because it allows him to receive rewards and to avoid being punished.[20] Finding such behavior to his advantage, the child carries it with him into adulthood. This theory, although a minority view, may explain the acts of Berkowitz, whose adoptive parents indulged him by granting his every wish. This type of parenting may have given him his spoiled, childlike personality, which he was never able to outgrow.

Whether psychopathy and aggressive behavior result more from parental neglect or overindulgence is subject to further debate. What seems clear from all of these theories, however, is that, if parents are abusive, ineffectual, or inconsistent in their discipline, their offspring are much more likely to display psychopathic, antisocial behavior. This is especially true of the child who develops into a secondary psychopath, for, as we have seen in Chapter 4, this type of individual exhibits antisocial behavior because of underlying emotional stress.[21]

Because of the unstable, inadequate, and often violent homelife of serial murderers, the above theories on aggression and psychopathy apply to them as well. It seems that they, too, learned their aggressive and abusive behavior from the role models their parents projected, while others turned to antisocial conduct as a result of their parents' inability to provide a nurturing environment. In either case, these eventual violent killers grew up in a world where love and compassion were all but absent for them. Although this deficiency served to foster their later aggressive behavior, it cannot stand alone to explain what motivates the serial murderer, since many individuals who were abused or neglected as children never commit such crimes.

Intense Frustration

Another consequence of the serial murderer's inadequate homelife is his inability to learn how to cope with failures. Throughout adolescence and adulthood the serial killer attempts to reach many goals without knowing how to deal with the disappointments along the way. When he does encounter failure at work or with a relationship, it thus has a traumatic and lasting effect, thereby causing intense frustration and a lowering of his already shallow sense of self-worth. This raises still another theory on why the serial murderer kills; it states that his actions are caused by intense, inner frustration.

With most people, frustration may result from numerous causal factors, including personal failures and limitations, interpersonal or material loss, lack of resources (for example, finances), feelings of guilt, and loneliness. However, with the serial murderer, his constant failures at life's endeavors continuously frustrate his desire to be successful. As each setback causes more frustration, he experiences an increasing sense of inner turmoil. Abrahamsen notes this phenomenon, explaining that the inner conflicts displayed by serial murderers originate in childhood and build in intensity throughout life. Several other researchers agree that the backgrounds of many of these individuals include a life punctuated by numerous and varied intense frustrations.[22]

Moreover, this constant buildup of tension culminates in extremely high levels of anxiety and frustration, which are often seen immediately before a murder is committed. Lasting from several hours to several weeks, this mounting tension eventually erupts in an act of brutal violence. Levin and Fox note that this behavior is a common and recurrent theme throughout the lives of multiple killers. Indeed, Benjamin Karpman suggests that all of the antisocial behavior of the secondary psychopath can be traced as well to frustration, or to some type of emotional deprivation.[23] Thus, the serial murderer may commit his crimes in part because of this buildup of intense frustration. When it reaches unbearable proportions, the killer may find it necessary to seek release through the act of murder.

The frustration buildup theory is similar to what Freud called the psychodynamic, or hydraulic, model. He was convinced that from birth human beings are constantly susceptible to a buildup of "aggressive energy," which must be released periodically before it reaches dangerous levels, much like the pressure in a container must be relieved to prevent it from exploding. Freud suggested that violent behavior and murder are manifestations of this aggressive energy discharge and termed this process *catharsis*.[24]

This theory of frustration, or aggressive energy, buildup seems quite valid, since almost all serial killers exhibit extreme amounts of tension and frustration. Berkowitz clearly explained that he became more cold-blooded as his frustrations built on a daily basis,[25] and Kemper as well suffered from intense levels of frustration. It is interesting that he even described the killing of his mother as a cathartic experience, alluding to the very theory Freud had suggested.[26]

In further support of this theory is the pattern of killing exhibited by the serial murderer, who tends to develop a methodic, regular interval between his crimes in which his tension initially subsides but then returns. His attacks therefore seem to result from a cyclical pattern of building frustration. With each act the frustration is relieved but only for a short time, after which it, or aggressive energy, begins to build again, requiring another murder. Berkowitz himself relates that the mounting tension within him was completely relieved when he committed his first murder, but it soon resurfaced.[27]

Freud's theory of catharsis also postulates that aggressive energy may be relieved by actual behavior or vicariously. If this is so, it may be that the serial killer first relieves his built-up frustrations vicariously through the violent fantasy world that he has created. When these fantasies fail to alleviate his increasing tension and frustration, he may at that point turn to actual murder. Although this theory seems highly plausible, there are many researchers who disagree with the Freudian model, asserting that the available evidence to date indicates that frustration eventually dissipates even without an aggressive act.[28]

In part as a response to this criticism, Freud's original proposition has been modified and a revised frustration-aggression theory established. In this version, it is argued that frustration does not always lead to aggression but merely increases the probability that an individual will soon act aggressively. It is believed that aggression is only one common response to frustration, with other reactions being withdrawal, doing nothing, or trying to alter the situation by a more compromising approach. An individual's reaction to frustration will therefore depend upon prior learning and personal differences.[29]

Even though Freud's original theory has been modified in this way, it still provides an explanation for serial murder as the result of mounting tension. Since the serial killer never learns how to cope with frustration, he is more vulnerable to its unexpected effects than the average person.[30] Moreover, because he was taught that aggressive behavior is an appropriate way to alleviate frustration, an aggressive act may be the only way he knows how to release this overwhelming feeling. With either version of the Freudian model, the serial murderer kills to relieve overpowering anxiety and tension.

At this point the reader may be puzzled as to why this psychoanalytic theory is presented as a sociological explanation for serial murder. The answer lies in the fact that the frustrations experienced by the killer, thus prompting his aggressive behavior, are predominantly caused by environmental factors resulting from failures in familial, social, and interpersonal contacts. Therefore, it now must be determined what these sociological factors are and what triggers this intense frustration within the serial killer.

As previously discussed, one cause is the parents' inconsistent or violent behavior, which creates an atmosphere of uncertainty and unpredictability in the child's life. When he engages in a specific activity, he may at varying times either be praised or reprimanded. When he finds that he can never please his parents, this confuses and frustrates the child and can have a profound effect upon his well-being.

Another source of frustration lies in the serial murderer's continual failure at interpersonal contacts, since he was never taught how to develop a warm, close relationship with another person. This can be an incredibly frustrating experience, for not only does he yearn for a meaningful relationship, but he also sees others enjoying what he is incapable of achieving. It is therefore easy to understand how he never overcomes his inadequate sense of self-worth or his lack of self-confidence.

A third cause of frustration for the serial killer is his repeated failure in school, the military, and employment. As previously noted, the serial murderer's performance in these areas is often poor, despite his high intelligence and potential. His many attempts to achieve success often fall short of his desired goals, and this as well has a debilitating effect upon his self-esteem and adds to the already mounting frustration. Thus, the serial murderer experiences a tremendous amount of frustration throughout his life because of his inability to perform as others do in society. Many in the field believe that this is a key contributing factor in the development of the serial killer, although, as we shall see in Chapter 7, it is not the only important element at work in his formation.

Need for Power

So far, one basic theme seems to prevail throughout the lives of most serial murderers. What they most want to accomplish they find unattainable, the person they desire to be they discover they will never become, and the life-style they wish to maintain is never realized. Since the serial murderer therefore seeks a sense of power and control that his life otherwise lacks, he achieves this end by killing others.[31]

It is generally recognized by many researchers that aggressive behavior helps an individual to control the environment around him. Levin and Fox, for instance, maintain that the pleasure experienced by the serial killer from his repeated acts of murder comes from the complete dominance he exercises over his victim.[32] This need to prevail over others results from his feelings of powerlessness, worthlessness, and lack of self-fulfillment, which he trys to counteract by controlling, manipulating, or eliminating those who are vulnerable. Thus, according to this theory, the serial killer's repeated crimes are committed in an attempt to achieve some sense of control, since he grew up in an environment in which he was virtually powerless.[33]

Ronald Holmes and James DeBurger identify this need for power as a strong motivational force behind the acts of the lust murderer, explaining that, in addition to the sexual release, the killer experiences a great surge of triumph with each attack. Thus, the lust murderer seems motivated not only by his sexual desires but also by his craving for power. It is pointed out, however, that the feeling of power experienced disappears after a short time, and the killer then must seek out another victim in order to regain his sense of control.[34] If this same process is at work within the serial murderer, it is clear then why he resorts to repeated acts of violence.

This motivational force also has been recognized for many years as a strong component in certain acts of rape, whereby power is the paramount factor behind the offender's acts. Using the term "power rape" to describe these assaults, researchers explain that the offender's intent is not to harm his victim but to dominate him or her sexually. Having no control over his own life, he attempts to compensate for his inadequacies and helplessness by expressing mastery, strength, and authority over another. The act of rape for this individual does not satisfy any sexual needs but rather allows him to feel strong, powerful, and in control.[35]

In addition to power rapists, researchers note that child molesters are motivated in part by a need to exercise social control. Sex with a child allows them to achieve this dominance, since the child will be passive and submissive during the encounter.[36] Likewise, necrophiliacs are believed to prefer sex with a corpse because of the complete control they have over their dead partners. Thus, the need for power is clearly a strong motivational force in many crimes of violent assault.

This theory seems to apply to the serial murderer, since it is evident in many of the case histories we have examined. Detectives interviewing Bundy after his arrest in Florida discovered that he had killed women because he needed to possess and dominate them. Ann Rule also maintains that Bundy's crimes were not sexually motivated but rather were committed because he wanted to humiliate and demean his victims, thereby achieving control over them. Bundy himself said that the gratification for serial killers lies not in the violent or sexual aspect of the assault but in the possession of the victim.[37] Similarly, this need for power was believed to be a motivational force behind Gacy's crimes. As an adult, those who knew him discovered that he wanted to dominate everyone around him. When his efforts were thwarted because of his personal and social inabilities, his murders became the ultimate expression of control, since he could torture his victims to the verge of death yet maintain the power to let them live. Indeed, some suggest that Gacy found much more gratification in this aspect of his killings than from any sexual pleasure.[38]

Further examples include Berkowitz, who, as a child, set many small fires. Not being detected at these acts gave him a strong sense of power over his environment. This quest for power continued into adulthood, where resorting to murder was his attempt to enhance his self-esteem by achieving dominance over women. Those involved with the case observed that, although he admitted to being nervous during his first murder, after each subsequent crime he often ran back to his car feeling flushed by the power he had had over his victim.[39]

Kemper as well enjoyed the sense of power he experienced through his crimes, since they allowed him to possess his victims, thereby controlling their fate. And, during his several marriages, Buono always tried to dominate his wives completely. Lucas, too, had an exaggerated need to feel powerful and important. Likewise, when police questioned DeSalvo about his crimes, he explained that he felt powerful when he could make his victims submit to his wishes.[40]

It is apparent that this personality trait is an important factor behind the serial murderer's acts. Levin and Fox maintain that this need for power underlies every aspect of the serial killer's life and is evident in his fascination with powerful automobiles, police and military uniforms, weapons, and instruments of torture.[41] This theory explains the serial murderer's recognizable characteristic as a "police groupie," the high-speed chases he leads, and his fits of rage when he does not get his own way.

Elliot Leyton, in examining the crimes of Kemper, dismisses the idea that he murdered his victims because of a need to possess them, arguing instead that this was merely a contrived explanation by Kemper's attorney designed to obtain a favorable sentence. Rather, Leyton believes that Kemper's crimes, as well as the acts of all serial murderers, are a campaign of revenge directed against the social class from which they have been excluded. He points to the fact that serial killers, although ambitious social climbers, never achieve that place in society to which they aspire. Therefore, he concludes that it is this unrealizable ambition that motivates them to a form of social war against the upper classes.[42]

Leyton's theory, however, fails to account for serial murderers, such as Buono and Bianchi, who, by attacking prostitutes, killed women from a lower social class. In addition, Corona, a successful businessman, took the lives of migrant workers who were obviously of a lower class. Moreover, Lucas and Toole killed numerous people from a wide range of social groups. Accordingly, it is not the case that serial killers murder only those from a higher social rank. This does not mean, however, that Leyton's theory is completely wrong. Rather, his conclusions are merely a narrower view of the idea that the serial murderer kills to achieve the power in his life that he has otherwise been denied.

It is clear, then, that the serial killer's need for a sense of power plays an extremely important role in the motivational force behind his crimes. Finding that committing murder gives him an intense feeling of control over others, he repeats his act, since it is the only means of achieving that end. We shall see in Chapter 7 just how significant this theory is in explaining serial murder.

Undercontrolled or Overcontrolled Behavior

Another theory that attempts to explain violent behavior in general identifies two distinct personalities: the undercontrolled and the overcontrolled aggressive types. The undercontrolled individual has very low inhibitors against his aggressive nature and frequently engages in violence, as a result of never having been taught to restrain his antisocial behavior.[43] Consequently, whenever he is frustrated, his response is an aggressive one. Although he is not completely unable to control his violence, and does not exhibit wild fits of rage, his ability to suppress anger is severely impaired. Because of this he is often diagnosed as a sociopathic personality. The overcontrolled type is the exact opposite and has learned to suppress his aggressive tendencies to extremes. Indeed, no matter what the provocation this individual will not respond assertively until the buildup of tension within finally reaches a point where some minor irritation is all that is needed to bring about a catastrophic, explosive act of violence.[44]

It is suggested by several researchers that the more brutal slayings are often performed by the normally inhibited, overcontrolled individual. Using a theory similar to Freud's psychodynamic model, they postulate that, since the undercontrolled releases his tension periodically, his level of frustration never rises to extremes and therefore his aggressive behavior is not explosively violent. In contrast, the overcontrolled's frustration level reaches overwhelming proportions before his pent-up hostility is finally released in one violent and brutal antisocial act.[45] Thus, his crimes are usually much worse in intensity (rape or murder, for example) compared to those of the undercontrolled, who commits many more but of a lesser degree—that is, fighting, burglary, or constant assaultive behavior.

Although this theory may have some validity generally, as applied to the serial killer it is questionable. The serial murderer, because he closely resembles the psychopath, would be classified as an undercontrolled aggressive type, since this theory would group the psychopath as such.[46] His manipulative and usually outgoing nature, as well as his repeated crimes, places him within the ambit of the undercontrolled offender. Because he suffers from extreme levels of frustration, however, that result in a violent burst of aggression, the serial murderer is also much like the overcontrolled individual. He therefore takes on the characteristics of both personalities.

If this theory is to be used to explain serial murder, it must be that the serial killer is not solely of either type. Indeed, it is recognized by supporters of this theory that the two types are not mutually exclusive. Although most offenders are of one or the other, many lie somewhere in between.[47] Accordingly, the serial murderer may commit his acts because of a combination of overcontrolled and undercontrolled behavior. He might suppress his frustration, just as the overcontrolled individual does, while at other times express it in inappropriate ways—for instance, through petty property crimes, voyeurism, or assaultive behavior—similar to the undercontrolled.

This theory of overcontrolled versus undercontrolled behavior, when compared to those already discussed, seems merely to be a reiteration of the frustration theories examined earlier. It adds no new information to the search for the cause of serial murder. Additionally, because the serial killer's acts are attributable to a combination of overcontrolled and undercontrolled behaviors, a problem with relying upon this is apparent. Almost all individuals in society exhibit the characteristics of either overcontrolled or undercontrolled behavior. Indeed, everyone differs in his or her ability to deal with frustration, with some having a low tolerance level and others possessing a high one. In addition, any one person's ability to handle a frustrating situation may vary at times. Yet these individuals do not turn to murder, and most never even commit a crime. It is therefore clear that this theory, by itself, cannot provide an answer to the question of what motivates the serial killer. Although he does suffer from a tremendous amount of built-up frustration throughout his life, which is an important component of his later murderous acts, it alone is not the explanation for serial murder.

Excitement of the Hunt

Still another theory holds out that the murder itself is not the incentive for the crime at all. Rather, the motivating force lies in the exhilaration felt by the serial killer as he stalks his victim, anticipating and fantasizing about his impending act. As already seen, he often devotes countless hours roaming the streets in search of a victim. Berkowitz, for example, has acknowledged that "cruising" was always a vital part of his ritualistic activity, and Bundy as well explained the importance of the hunt for his prey. In discussing a hypothetical killer, he said that the pursuit provides a high degree of excitement and arousal.[48] There is no pleasure received from harming the person attacked; instead, the satisfaction comes from the fantasy that accompanies and fuels the anticipation preceding each crime. What really becomes a strong motivational force is the hunt and subsequent possession of his victims, both of which give him a strong feeling of power over them and his environment.[49]

The fact that the serial killer derives excitement from anticipating the capture of his victim does not explain, however, why he is motivated to carry out the murder once the hunt is over. The answer lies in the earlier explanation of the killer's need for power. By committing an act of murder, he perpetuates and even increases the sense of power and control over his victims that he obtained throughout the pursuit.

Societal Roles

A further theory attributes the serial killer's acts in part to the roles that men and women are supposed to fulfill in society. Traditionally, men must be strong, powerful, and unemotional while women are weak and submissive. If an individual does not fit into his expected role, he is often ridiculed or rejected. He then may experience anxiety and frustration because of his second-class status. Although he may attempt to conform to society's values, he may never attain that level of behavior which it has preordained for him.

The serial killer, who often feels powerless and weak, thus may commit his violent crimes because of extreme pressures placed on him, both psychological and sociological, to live up to the societal role he perceives he is expected to fulfill. Indeed, Abrahamsen attributes much of the frustration experienced by the serial murderer to the American ideal that men must be strong and "manly" in order to be successful, since it is precisely this virility that the killer lacks. Moreover, many believe that a large percentage of crime in general is the result of the criminal's inability to meet societal standards. As explained by one research team, society leads most of us to desire material items and respect yet denies to many the opportunity to attain these goals. This denial may result in robbery to obtain material goods and violence to earn respect.[50] In the case of the serial killer, he ultimately turns to murder as a means of acquiring that which he has not been allowed.

Media Influence and Pornography

A final sociological theory suggests that the media play an important role in stimulating serial murder, as well as in shaping an individual's behavior. Indeed, commercial and political interests invest heavily in advertising in an attempt to influence the public.[51] Researchers generally believe that when violence is seen in the media, especially on television, it has a very strong impact on many viewers. Just what this impact is, however, is the subject of a raging debate.

It is suggested that any one of three results is possible from being exposed to television violence: 1) the restraint over violent acts is weakened, thereby increasing such crimes; 2) an excitement and stimulation of violent ideas, which also prompts aggression; or 3) a reduction of violent behavior by allowing the viewer to express his aggression vicariously through the acts of those on the screen.[52] Numerous studies have been conducted to test these alternatives as well as the overall effects of televised violence on the viewer. Sadly, however, none shows conclusively what these consequences are, and most reach divergent conclusions and contradict one another in many ways. Some propose a minimal causal relationship between television violence and aggression while others boast of a direct correlation.[53] The end result is a wealth of confusing data with no reliable consensus of opinion.

One of the better studies, however, begun in 1960, is the Rip Van Winkle Study, which initially recorded the viewing habits and behavior of 875 third grade children in upstate New York.

Ten years later these individuals were again examined. After comparing the results, researchers discovered that early signs of aggression, especially in males, are highly predictive of later violence; children who are the most aggressive watch the most television; and persons with a lower IQ are more likely to be aggressive. From these findings, they concluded that watching television from an early age helps cause hostile behavior, independent of intelligence, parents' occupations, parental discipline, or even the amount of viewing hours. In addition, boys with low IQs are more likely to be aggressive, since they tend to spend more time getting lost in the world of television.[54] Conversely, however, other studies have found very little, if any, correlation. These surveys conclude that, although televised violence "may be related" to aggressive behavior, its impact is small and the actual aggression expressed is extremely diverse.[55]

It is apparent, then, that the long-term results of televised violence on the viewer's behavior is the subject of much debate, and no one conclusion is universally accepted. Thus, it is impossible to test how it affects the development of the serial murderer. A growing number of researchers, however, agree that observed violence does significantly affect short-term hostility. As an example, they point out that a crowd of teenagers, after seeing a violent movie, is more likely to leave the theater and start a fight in the streets. Another example might be one in which, while viewing a football game, a spectator punches a fan from the other team because of the aggression displayed on the field. Using these incidences to support their proposition, these researchers believe that the clearest impact that the media has on its viewers is that some people imitate specific newsworthy events that they have seen on television.[56] In this way, the news media play an important role in the short-term aggressive behavior exhibited by certain individuals.

This short-term media influence is also evident when a murderer obtains the idea for his criminal act after seeing or reading reports of other killings. These descriptions remain prominent in the mind of the prospective killer, who replays the scenarios again and again until they become the script for his own murderous acts.[57] This type of copycat behavior is present in serial killers as well. As previously noted, Corll, Henley, and Brooks killed twenty-seven young boys in Houston, Texas, over a three-year period. Accounts of their methods of torture were printed in many newspapers across the country in 1973. Shortly thereafter, Gacy used some of the exact same techniques on his victims. There can be little doubt that the detailed media coverage of the Texas slayings contributed to Gacy's crimes.

Thus, violence in the media does play a role in the short-term aggression exhibited by serial murderers as well as the general public. Virtually no conclusive evidence, however, has been formulated on the long-term effects of televised violence. The various studies written on the subject reach very different results and provide no clear answers. Moreover, none appears to exist on the long-term effects of media violence on serial murder. Accordingly, sole reliance on this theory leaves many unanswered questions.

Another subject of much debate is the influence of pornography. As already seen, the serial murderer usually is intrigued with, and has an insatiable appetite for, pornographic materials. In fact, many researchers assert that he derives his ideas about torture and domination of women and children from the submissive roles that these individuals often assume in sadistic and pornographic literature. In addition, it is believed that these depictions of the aggressive, violent male not only originate violent ideas within the serial killer but also provide the impetus for many of his sadistic fantasies.

In 1986 a commission set up by the U.S. attorney general released a report on the effects of pornography on society. After conducting exhaustive research and special hearings on the subject, the commission concluded that substantial exposure to sexually violent materials has a causal relationship to antisocial acts of sexual violence. More specifically, it found that exposure to obscene, erotic literature and aggressiveness toward women were directly correlated.[58] The commission also discovered that even nonviolent pornography promoted this same behavior toward the opposite sex, since women were often portrayed in a degrading, humiliating, or subordinate role. Consequently, exposure to this type of material might lead one to view rape or other forms of forced sexual acts as less serious, the victims as more responsible, and the offenders as less accountable.[59]

Another effect of pornography on the offender is noted by Dr. Gene Abel, who testified before the attorney general's commission. He relates that, once an individual begins to engage in deviant behavior, that person uses pornography as a means of sustaining fantasies of his crimes in between the actual acts. In this way the offender prolongs the sense of arousal he experienced during the crime by reliving it through fantasy. Abel explains that this fantasy initially reduces the risk of further crime, but, because it extends the aroused state, it increases the chances of more violence over time. He thus concludes that, when sex offenders employ pornography to reduce their physical urges temporarily, over the long term there is a likelihood of heightened antisocial behavior.[60]

It is clear, then, that many researchers, as well as the attorney general's commission, see both violent and nonviolent pornography as harmful to society. Many others, however, strongly question this view, criticizing the attorney general's report and pointing out that its conclusions rest largely on assumptions rather than on concrete evidence. It is argued by opponents that actual research shows absolutely no causal relationship between violent sexual materials and sexual aggression.[61] Indeed, the commission itself cautioned that further study must be conducted before a definitive answer on the full effects of pornography can be reached.[62]

Whether pornography causes, or even contributes to, actual violent behavior will no doubt remain the subject of heated debate for some time. Assuming that it promotes violent behavior, however, it may be that it does so to a much greater extent with the serial killer. Given his immature development, pornographic material may produce a more drastic and lasting impact upon his later behavior than upon other members of society. Moreover, the violence depicted in such literature may take the place of normal sexual encounters because of his inability to experience mature relationships. This in turn conditions him to seek out more violent and aggressive expressions of his sexuality than otherwise would be sought, and he then comes to rely upon pornography as the script for his behavior. In fact, just prior to his execution, Bundy admitted that violent sexual literature had been a tremendous influence in the formation of his murderous behavior.[63] The existence of pornography, therefore, appears to play a significant role in the motivation of those who commit serial murder.

There are obviously a number of sociological explanations that attempt to account for the acts of the serial murderer. Many of these discussed in this chapter overlap and complement psychological explanations, while others are closely aligned with those in the field of biology. Thus, our inquiry now turns to the biological theories of aggression and murder.

Notes

1. Wilson and Herrnstein at 213–62; Leehan and Wilson at 3–25; Lunde at 96; Finkelhor at 357.
2. Wilson and Herrnstein at 254–56; Burgess et al. at 261; Rogers and Terry at 95–97.
3. Leehan and Wilson at 3.
4. Id. at 18–19.
5. Bartol at 190 (citing to Albert Bandura, *Aggression: A Social Learning Analysis* [Englewood Cliffs, NJ: Prentice-Hall, 1973]).
6. Lunde at 15, 24; Wilson and Herrnstein at 227–29; Siegel and Senna at 261–63.
7. Wilson and Herrnstein at 227.
8. Bartol at 221 (citing to Hans Toch, *Violent Men: An Inquiry into the Psychology of Violence* [Chicago: Aldine, 1969]).
9. Bartol at 221.
10. Wilson and Herrnstein at 229.
11. Id. at 230 (citing to Gerald R. Patterson, *Coercive Family Process* [Eugene, OR: Castalia, 1982]).
12. Wilson and Herrnstein at 230–31.
13. Bartol at 96 (citing to Leonard Berkowitz, *Aggression: A Social-Psychological Analysis* [New York: McGraw-Hill, 1962]; Leonard Berkowitz, "The Frustration-Aggression Hypothesis Revisited," in *Roots of Aggression*, ed. Leonard Berkowitz [New York: Atherton Press, 1969]: 1–28).
14. Wilson and Herrnstein at 223 (citing to Michael Rutter, *Maternal Deprivation Reassessed* [New York: Penguin Books, 1972]).
15. Abrahamsen (1973); Bartol; Lunde; and Rule.
16. Bartol at 79–82.
17. Id. at 80 (citing to Arnold H. Buss, *Psychopathology* [New York: Wiley, 1966]).
18. Bartol at 80 (citing to William McCord and Joan McCord, *The Psychopath: An Essay on the Criminal Mind* [Princeton, NJ: Van Nostrand, 1964]).
19. Bartol at 81; Cleckley at 411.
20. Bartol at 81 (citing to E. J. Phares, "A Social Learning Theory Approach to Psychopathology," in Julian B. Rotter, J. Chana, and E. J. Phares, eds., *Applications of a Social Learning Theory of Personality* [New York: Holt, Rinehart and Winston, 1972]).
21. Bartol at 81; Karpman at 118, 135.

22. Abrahamsen (1973) at 9, 13, 240. See also Bartol at 225 (citing to Berkowitz, *Aggression: A Social-Psychological Analysis*; Stuart Palmer, *Psychology of Murder* [New York: Thomas Crowell, 1960]; Andrew F. Henry and James F. Short, *Suicide and Homicide* [Glencoe, IL: Free Press, 1954]).

23. Lunde at 97; Levin and Fox at 68; Karpman at 135.

24. Bartol at 181.

25. Abrahamsen (1985) at 102.

26. From an interview conducted for the film *Murder: No Apparent Motive*.

27. Abrahamsen (1985) at 178, 204.

28. Bartol at 182. See also id. at 97–98 (citing to William E. Broen, *Schizophrenia: Research and Theory* [New York: Academic Press, 1968]).

29. Id. at 186–87.

30. Id. at 95 (citing to Berkowitz, *Aggression: A Social-Psychological Analysis*).

31. Holmes and DeBurger (1985) at 32–33; id. (1988) at 99–100; Egger at 304; House of Rep. Hearing at 18–19.

32. Bartol at 192; Levin and Fox at 68; Egger at 30.

33. Levin and Fox at 68 (citing to Erich Fromm, *The Anatomy of Human Destructiveness* [New York: Holt, Rinehart and Winston, 1973]). See also Levin and Fox at 72; Egger at 304; and MacDonald at 103–4.

34. Holmes and DeBurger (1988) at 99.

35. *Encyclopedia of Crime and Justice* at 1353.

36. Craft at 72.

37. Larsen at 233; Rule at 341; Michaud and Aynesworth at 23.

38. Sullivan and Maiken at 242, 338, 235; Egger at 183.

39. Abrahamsen (1985) at 42, 182, 108, 192; Leyton at 157.

40. Egger at 214, 256; Frank at 314; Leyton at 140.

41. Levin and Fox at 70.

42. Leyton at 62, 26–27, 294.

43. Bartol at 221–22.

44. Lester at 102; Bartol at 222.

45. Bartol at 222–23 (citing to Edwin I. Megargee, "Undercontrolled and Overcontrolled Personality Types in Extreme Antisocial Aggression," *Psychological Monographs* 80 [March 1966]: 1–29; Ronald Blackburn, "Personality in Relation to Extreme Aggression in Psychiatric Offenders," *British Journal of Psychiatry* 114 [July 1968]: 821–28; Joe P. Tupin, Dennis Mahar, and David Smith, "Two Types of Violent Offenders with Psychosocial Descriptors," *Diseases of the Nervous System* 34 [October-November 1973]: 356–63; Melvin Lee, Philip G. Zimbardo, and Minerva Bertholf, "Shy Murderers," *Psychology Today* 11 [November 1977]: 68–70).

46. Id. at 222.

47. Id. at 224.

48. Abrahamsen (1985) at 93. See also note 15, Chapter 4.

49. Michaud and Aynesworth at 123.

50. Levin and Fox at 53; Abrahamsen (1985) at xii; Wilson and Herrnstein at 214–15.

51. Wilson and Herrnstein at 337.

52. Id. at 338; Donnerstein et al. at 133.

53. Wilson and Herrnstein at 340–54; Wilson (Paul) at 53–56.

54. Wilson and Herrnstein at 344 (citing to Leonard D. Eron et al., "Does Television Violence Cause Aggression?" *American Psychologist* 27 [April 1972]: 253–63).

55. Id. at 353 (citing to National Academy of Sciences/National Research Council, *News Report*, March 1983).

56. Wilson and Herrnstein at 348, 353.

57. Id. at 348; Bartol at 192.

58. *Attorney General's Commission on Pornography* at 326, 324; Donnerstein et al. at 87.

59. *Attorney General's Commission on Pornography* at 332.

60. Minnery at 151–52.

61. Nobile and Nader at 233–39.

62. *Attorney General's Commission on Pornography* at 349–50.

63. "Bundy Executed" at 10.

6 Biological Explanations

The human physiology is a vast network of complex formations and structures. Its intricacies often both amaze and confound medical science. One of the least understood areas of this perplexing network is the human brain. It still is, in large part, a mystery to modern scientists as to its function and influence over human behavior. A number of researchers have attempted to identify structures or processes within the brain that have a direct link to aggressive, violent behavior. As with psychological and sociological theories, however, there is no one clear biological explanation. Yet, the research available to date does suggest a connection between physiology and aggression. Although there seem to be no studies on the physiological characteristics of the serial murderer specifically, several studies have been done on the physiology of aggressive individuals in general. Their results are examined in this chapter and related to the serial murderer in an attempt to shed light upon the motivation behind his acts.

Retardation in the Development of the Brain

One explanation for aggressiveness suggests that violent behavior occurs as a result of retardation in brain development. In the hope of finding some support for this theory, electroencephalogram (EEG) readings of aggressive individuals have been evaluated. In one study, researchers, after excluding those with epilepsy, mental subnormality, or a history of major head injury, compared prisoners who were habitually aggressive with others who had committed single, major violent crimes.[1] They found that the incidence of EEG abnormali-

ties was 57 percent in the former group, compared to 12 percent
in the latter. Interestingly, in the chronically aggressive group,
the abnormalities were almost always seen over the anterior part
of the brain, suggesting a malfunction in the area of the temporal
lobes.[2] This is of particular note since a portion of the temporal
lobe is associated with emotion, personality, and behavior as a
result of its connection to the limbic and frontal lobes. Other
research findings as well tend to corroborate these results.[3]

In another study the EEG readings of sixty-four individuals
charged with murder were examined and compared. Here it was
found that those who acted under considerable provocation had
an abnormal EEG rate of 17 percent, those who killed acciden-
tally while committing some other crime had a 25 percent abnormality rate, explosive psychopaths who acted without motive
or provocation showed a 73 percent rate, while the highest rate of
86 percent occurred in those who were psychotic.[4]

Other findings on the EEG readings of violent psychopaths
reveal a similar pattern of abnormality. Several researchers have
noted that those of the psychopath are of a slow-wave variety,
delta and theta waves, whereas control groups of nonpsychopaths
exhibit normal alpha and beta waves.[5] These abnormal EEG
readings do not take the place of normal patterns but seem to be
intermixed with regular brain-wave activity, thereby making
them different from the slow-wave readings exhibited by individuals who suffer from head injury or some types of tumors.
Rather, these slow waves generally indicate immature brain
activity, since these closely resemble the EEG results of children.[6]

In a study of 194 aggressive psychopaths, abnormalities in
EEG readings all indicated some type of maturational defect in
cerebral organization and function, thereby supporting the proposal of a maturational retardation hypothesis that maintains
that the brain and cortical functioning of the psychopath are
immature and childlike.[7] This theory is used to account for the
behavioral patterns exhibited by the psychopath, such as self-
centeredness, impulsiveness, and an inability to delay gratification, all of which are characteristic of the behavior of children.

What is of particular interest in studying the EEG patterns of
psychopaths is that many of the abnormalities tend to diminish
and even completely disappear with increasing age, and the
previously immature brain-wave activity develops into an es-

sentially normal, mature pattern over time.[8] This process usually occurs between the ages of thirty and forty, thereby indicating that there is a delay in the physiological development in certain areas of the psychopath's brain and accounting for his childish ways and inability to exhibit normal emotional responses to various stimuli. It also helps to explain why the psychopath's antisocial behavior tends to lessen substantially after age thirty.[9] By that time, the developmental lag within the brain structures, for some unknown reason, has been corrected.

The serial murderer as well may suffer from some form of maturational retardation, since he exhibits many of the immature characteristics displayed by the psychopath: sexual immaturity, emotional impotency, erratic bursts of temper, and an inability to maintain interpersonal relationships. Indeed, Berkowitz and Bundy both had the emotional maturity of a twelve-year-old. Moreover, as already seen, most serial killers are between the ages of twenty and thirty-five. This finding may be indicative of a maturation of the serial murderer's brain after age thirty-five, for once it reaches normal maturity levels, he is better equipped to handle emotional problems in a more mature, socially acceptable manner, as opposed to expressing his feelings through violent, aggressive acts.

One must be cautious, however, in drawing such broad conclusions. EEG studies must first be conducted on known serial murderers before any definitive hypothesis can be formulated. Since differences exist between the psychopath and the serial killer, the data obtained through studies on the psychopath may not be entirely applicable to the serial murderer; for example, both Bundy and Gacy had essentially normal EEG readings. Moreover, it is claimed by some that serial murderers never "grow out of" their violent behavior. On the contrary, it is believed that they will continue to kill even when they are well into their forties and fifties.[10]

In addition, many researchers dispute the assertion that abnormal EEG readings and psychopathic behavior are related, firmly maintaining that there is no significant correlation between the two.[11] In criticizing those studies that find such a connection, they assert that, if a distinction is not made between anterior temporal lobe epilepsy and midtemporal lobe epilepsy,[12] it is easy to discover EEG abnormalities in the temporal lobes of psychopaths. Moreover, if one distinguishes between psychomotor epileptics and psychopaths, the incidence of temporal lobe disorders is considerably reduced. Thus, this is a controversial theory as applied to the psychopath, and even its proponents concede that more information is needed.[13]

As used to explain serial murder, the maturational retardation hypothesis is very limited. The lack of research data on the EEG readings of serial killers makes the application of this theory to our inquiry difficult. Moreover, because many researchers disagree as to whether there is any correlation between EEG abnormalities and aggressive behavior, reliance on this explanation, for the present, is misplaced. Although Bundy and Gacy, for instance, apparently had normal EEG readings, it has been discovered that abnormal electrical activity often occurs deep within the subcortical areas of the brain yet does not register on either cortical or scalp EEG sensors.[14] Thus, researchers need to conduct intensive testing on the EEG patterns of serial killers before it can be said definitively whether or not serial murder is caused by a retardation in brain development.

Stimulation-seeking Activity

It is also hypothesized that, physiologically, the psychopath does not receive the full impact of sensations from his environment. As a result, he must engage in greater and more exciting forms of behavior in order to obtain the optimal amount of stimulation necessary to keep the cerebral cortex "satisfied." This avenue of inquiry expands upon the stimulation-seeking hypothesis discussed in Chapter 4 and lends biological support to that theory. Proponents of this idea postulate that almost every individual seeks to maintain optimal levels of stimulation, in which "stimulation" refers to the amount of sensation or information processed by the cortex. Indeed, they argue that a large degree of any person's behavior can be explained in this way.[15] When the cortex becomes understimulated, the individual is prompted to seek more excitement. If, however, the cortex is somehow prevented from receiving a sufficient amount of stimulation, aggressive behavior may become necessary in some individuals.

Research to support this theory generally focuses upon an area of the brain known as the reticular activating system (RAS), which sometimes is called the arousal system and is the alerting system of the brain.[16] It consists of the reticular formation, subthalamus, hypothalamus, and medial thalamus, and it extends from the central core of the brain stem to all parts of the cerebral cortex. The RAS receives messages from neurons within the nervous system and communicates with the cerebral cortex. It underlies attentiveness to one's environment and acts as a sentinel that activates and maintains the general alertness of the cortex.[17]

The RAS, however, also has the ability to decrease cortical arousal. At times it blocks otherwise stimulating activity from reaching the cerebral cortex, which is then severely understimulated and underaroused. In discussing how this relates to the psychopath, Curtis Bartol, professor of psychology at Castleton State College (Vermont), explains that the RAS either does not activate the cortex sufficiently to receive incoming information or it adapts to the stimuli too quickly, thereby blocking out the needed stimulation to the brain. In either case, the psychopath is unable to reach optimal arousal levels and thus engages in thrill-seeking, antisocial behavior in order to attain satisfying cortical arousal.[18]

This process of an impaired RAS also may be at work in the serial murderer, whose antisocial, violent behavior results from the inability of other activities to provide adequate cortical stimulation. This explains why such a killer might turn to murder and why his crimes increase in intensity and frequency. After he commits his first few murders, his RAS already may have adapted to the stimulus and thus an increase in the intensity of the stimulating event must occur in order to maintain optimal arousal within the cortex.

Lending support to the idea that aggressiveness results from a malfunction of the RAS is the behavior and treatment of hyperactive children. Many believe that hyperactivity in childhood is a precursor for later antisocial behavior.[19] To combat this type of conduct, hyperactive children are often given stimulants. This seems an odd treatment method, since one expects such drugs to increase rather than decrease motor activity, thereby aggravating the child's hyperactivity. However, stimulants have the paradoxical effect of quelling hyperactive behavior, an anomaly that had baffled researchers for many years until the discovery of how the RAS functions. It is now thought that stimulants work to improve the efficiency of the RAS and other brain-stem structures. This enhanced operation allows more stimulation or information to reach the cortex and therefore decreases the need to seek further excitement. This in turn lessens the child's hyperactive behavior.[20] Thus, the efficiency of the RAS in processing and transmitting various stimuli seems to have a direct impact upon the hyperactive child's aggressive behavior.

The theory that an impairment of the RAS serves to increase aggressive behavior seems quite plausible, and some clinical and research studies tend to support this hypothesis. However, it is also used to explain the psychopath's inability to benefit from punishment in situations low in stimulation, such as prisons and classrooms.[21] If the serial murderer suffers from an impairment of the RAS, a similar inability to function in the essentially nonstimulating atmosphere of prison should exist. As we have seen, though, this is not the case. Gacy, for example, became a model prisoner, and Bundy enjoyed being enclosed, finding his prison cell more of a comfort than a punishment.[22] These observations offer contradictory evidence to the theory of a malfunctioning RAS, since the apparent stimulation-seeking and violent behavior of the serial killer notably declines when he is confined. Thus, a theory explaining serial murder as an effort to compensate for the underaroused cortex seems deficient.

This anomaly presents a stumbling block for the impaired RAS theory when it is applied to the serial murderer. We may speculate, however, as to why his violent behavior decreases while in prison and still rely upon a theory of an impaired RAS to explain his murderous acts. First, the RAS begins functioning normally, for some unknown reason, coincidentally or as a result of the murderer's incarceration. Second, the serial killer receives enormous attention and special treatment once in prison because of his infamy, or because of curiosity on the part of the public or other inmates, and this satisfies his increased need for stimulation. Finally, he may realize that no victims will be found in prison so he directs his stimulation-seeking activity, for example, toward becoming involved in legal battles of his case, as Bundy did, or pursuing other interests, such as becoming head chef, as did Gacy. In these ways, the need for stimulation, if it continues after incarceration, can be satisfied. These explanations, however, are only speculation, and much more research must be done in this area before this theory can be viewed as the complete answer to serial murder. Moreover, they do not account for the serial killer's initial choice of murder to satisfy his underaroused cortex as opposed to some other less violent activity.

The Thalamus, Hypothalamus, and Aggression

Focusing attention on the RAS has led researchers to discover that the pathways of the brain responsible for activation seem to involve both the thalamus and the hypothalamus. These two structures, which together make up an area of the brain known as the diencephalon, are suggested by many as having a direct relation to aggressive behavior.[23] The primary function of the thalamus is to serve as a relay center for processing sensory stimuli, such as pain, received by the brain. In addition, however, it plays a part in helping the individual to associate feelings of pleasantness or unpleasantness with sensory impulses. Reactions involved with the expression of emotions, such as rage or fear, are also influenced by this portion of the brain.[24] Thus, the thalamus performs a vital function in processing and interpreting a wide variety of stimuli as well as associating these with the appropriate emotional responses.

If there is a malfunction in the thalamus that consistently prevents certain emotion-provoking stimuli from being associated with human feeling, this may result in the individual's inability to understand or comprehend that which in others is a normal emotional response. Thus, he may display little or no reaction in an emotional situation. If the serial killer suffers from an impaired thalamus, this might explain his apparent lack of empathy for the pain he inflicts on others, as well as his inability to maintain any type of sustained relationship. He is simply physiologically incapable of experiencing the appropriate feelings.

Moreover, it may be that in the serial killer the thalamus incorrectly associates feelings of pleasantness with aggressive and violent sensory stimuli. In several experiments, researchers have shown that structures in the brain involved with oral and sexual functions (pleasant experiences) lie in close proximity to those concerned with fearful and combative behavior. When one area is stimulated, quite often the arousal spills over or "rebounds" into the adjoining area. Consequently, violent acts are associated with pleasurable feelings.[25] If the killer's thalamus improperly directs incoming stimuli in this way, he will be conditioned to find only violent activity pleasurable. After many years of this type of conditioning, it is easy to see how the serial murderer is directed toward such behavior.

The above theories, like those on the RAS, are predominantly speculative in nature when applied to serial murderers. Investigators have not been quick to pursue studies on the thalamus, and continued research is scarce. Moreover, no work has been done specifically to determine whether serial killers are motivated by improper thalamic function. Considerably more research, however, has focused upon the hypothalamus, which is the control center for regulating the body's most critical activities: food intake, endocrine levels, water balance, sexual rhythms, and the autonomic nervous system. It also manages a host of complex motivational states such as fatigue, hunger, anger, and placidity.[26]

In the late 1920s, Walter R. Hess, a Swiss professor of physiology, conducted an extensive series of tests in an effort to determine the function of the hypothalamus. After years of research, he discovered that there are two regions of the hypothalamus: the caudal, ergotropic region (concerned with excitation and sympathetic activation) and an anterior, trophotropic region (concerned with inhibition and parasympathetic responses). Furthermore, he found that when certain areas of the hypothalamus, particularly the ergotropic zone, were stimulated, aggressive behavior was consistently displayed.[27] Thus, he seemingly isolated the aggressive center of the brain.

Numerous studies followed Hess's original work, all confirming his findings. Of particular note is one study that concluded that two different types of aggression can be elicited depending upon where on the hypothalamus stimulation occurs. In general, it identified one area which, when stimulated, elicited violent, hostile outbursts of rage while the second provoked a more predatory, calculated form of aggression. It also found that the intensity of the stimulus needed to provoke aggression diminished as one progressed down through the hypothalamus.[28] Accordingly, the degree of violence used by the serial murderer also could depend upon the point of stimulation on the hypothalamus. If the lower portions are aroused, it is clear that the aggressive act carried out by the killer will be much more violent.

Although many believe that the hypothalamus is truly the brain's center for aggressive behavior, this theory also has its opponents. Indeed, many researchers continue to argue that aggressiveness cannot be predicted by focusing upon any one area of the brain; rather, they maintain that the brain is like a mosaic in which only the complete aggregate of seemingly unrelated parts will tell the whole story.[29] It is clear, then, that attention cannot rest solely upon a theory of a malfunctioning thalamus or hypothalamus when searching for the cause of aggression, since researchers are still debating about the importance of these structures. When the aggression displayed takes the form of serial murder, a total reliance on this theory is indeed misplaced. Although important discoveries have been made in the study of both structures, there is little scientific evidence to support the view that an impairment in either of these areas of the brain is the sole cause of violent, serial murder. Therefore, this theory cannot be the answer to what lies behind the serial killer's brutal acts.

Head Trauma

Another theory that relies upon a physiological explanation for murder maintains that violent behavior is the result of severe head injury. Several researchers assert that the past history of many violent criminals includes at least one instance where the individual suffered a severe blow to the head,[30] usually sustained as the result of a fall, an automobile accident, playground injury, or beatings received from parents.

In one study on the prevalence of head injuries in aggressive adults, researchers interviewed fifteen convicted murderers who were awaiting execution and questioned them at length regarding their medical histories.[31] If they claimed that they had suffered a head injury in the past, every effort was made to investigate such assertions by performing physical and neurological examinations, including EEG tests and CAT scans, as well as reviewing their hospital records and conducting interviews with family members. It was discovered that all fifteen murderers had a history of significant head injuries suffered in childhood or early adolescence. As a result, five of the subjects had neurological impairments, such as seizures, paralysis, or cortical degeneration, while seven others suffered from blackouts, dizziness, and psychomotor epileptic symptoms;[32] the remaining three, however, apparently had no obvious signs of brain malfunction. The researchers believed that this evidence should have been a mitigating factor for the trial courts in deciding whether to execute these individuals. Thus, they concluded that this physiological evidence of brain dysfunction due to head injury was an influential factor in the murders that were ultimately committed.

As an explanation for serial murder, this theory offers, at best, a limited answer. Although it is true that many serial killers suffered some type of severe head injury during childhood (for example, Gacy and Bianchi each experienced a playground accident, and Lucas was struck with a two-by-four by his mother), many others have no such history. In fact, their backgrounds are unremarkable in this respect. Moreover, thousands of children suffer from head accidents yet never develop violent tendencies. In addition, researchers note that, along with head injuries, most violent offenders have been physically abused or neglected as children.[33] As seen in Chapter 5, this alone can have a major impact on the future behavior of the child. It is therefore difficult to determine whether the violent behavior exhibited in later life is attributable to childhood head accidents or to deprivation. Although early head injuries may have some deleterious effects later on, they cannot be the sole reason for serial murder.

Neurotransmitters

Other researchers studying the biological causes of aggression focus not upon particular structures of the brain but upon chemicals produced in the body that affect those structures. Biologists, for instance, are beginning to study chemical substances known as neurotransmitters, which are directly involved in the transmission of neural impulses and seem to play a part in exciting or inhibiting aggressive behavior. Recent investigations have found that a number of neurotransmitters may influence the cortical and subcortical mechanisms responsible for aggression and violence.[34]

In researching neurotransmitters and aggression, researchers draw specific attention to a substance known as 5-hydroxyindoleacetic acid (5-HIAA), a metabolic by-product of the neurotransmitter serotonin. They have discovered that persistently aggressive animals have very low levels of both serotonin and 5-HIAA. Furthermore, some researchers note that this same condition exists in the spinal fluid of men who are aggressive or who demonstrate impulsive, antisocial behavior from childhood.[35] Low levels of serotonin and 5-HIAA also are found in individuals who attempt suicide. Of particular interest in this regard is the observation that the more violent suicides are committed by those with very little 5-HIAA.[36]

These findings seem to indicate a direct link between low levels of serotonin/5-HIAA and aggressive, violent behavior, although scientists have yet to determine whether lower amounts of these chemicals are a cause of, or result from, antisocial conduct. Moreover, the existing biological evidence to date suggests that no single neurotransmitter solely excites or inhibits aggression and violence. On the contrary, a variety of neurotransmitters can have this effect.[37] Thus, the only conclusion that can be drawn at this time is that aggressiveness and low levels of serotonin/5-HIAA seem to coexist. Since no studies have been conducted on the serotonin levels of serial killers, it is difficult to look to this theory as a cause of serial murder. It does, however, raise interesting questions for biologists and provides an avenue of research that should be pursued.

Heredity and Genetics

Still other researchers attempting to point to the cause of criminal behavior center upon heredity and genetics. It is now generally accepted that there is no such thing as a "crime gene." Although many at one time believed that the existence of an extra

Y chromosome, the XYY syndrome, caused violent behavior, this notion has been substantially undermined by scientific research. This does not mean, however, that heredity plays no part in criminal behavior. Many traits that are inheritable, such as intelligence and temperament, can influence the likelihood of later criminal behavior.[38]

To explore this notion of inherited criminal characteristics, investigators observed children who were separated at birth from their biological parents and later adopted. In a study concentrating on adopted males, it was discovered that these individuals were four times as likely to resort to crime if their biological parents (often traced through hospital and court records) engaged in criminal behavior. More specifically, the study found that if one parent is a property criminal—that is, a thief, burglar, or shoplifter—the male child most likely will become one as well, while the female child seldom will unless both parents were involved in such crimes.[39]

In a similar study, Sarnoff Mednick, a psychologist at the University of Southern California, corroborated these findings. After studying 14,427 Danish male adoptees, he found that the rate of criminal behavior was 13.5 percent when neither biological nor adoptive parents were criminals, 20 percent when only biological parents were criminals, and 24.5 percent in those cases in which both biological and adoptive parents engaged in crime.[40] Some maintain that these results clearly demonstrate that there is a connection between genetics and criminality. Others, however, are not so quick to reach such broad conclusions, asserting instead that what may be inherited are only genetic factors that influence the susceptibility to criminal behavior.[41]

Whether criminal behavior is ultimately pursued therefore will depend upon other contributing elements such as environment, social status, and family life. Researchers postulate that what may be inherited is actually a predisposition for fearlessness that, depending upon the individual's environment, manifests itself either as heroism or criminality.[42] Thus, what is inherited is not criminal behavior but aggressiveness, which is expressed in ways that are shaped by the environment.

Lending further support to this theory of inherited aggressiveness is a metabolic condition known as Lesch-Nyhan disease, which affects only males and is characterized by mental retardation, aggressive behavior, and self-mutilation. It is believed to result from excess uric acid production and is passed on from generation to generation.[43] It may be, therefore, that aggressiveness is inherited by the serial murderer. Indeed, we saw in Chapter 2 that Gacy's father was an extremely violent man, and Gacy himself is described as an exact reproduction of his father.[44] Both exhibited the same type of behavior, with Gacy, Sr., expressing his aggression through violence directed at his family, and Gacy, Jr., showing his by brutally attacking young men and boys.

Moreover, this inherited predisposition for risk-taking behavior helps to explain why the serial killer is often infatuated with police work, uniforms, and equipment. He may long to be a police officer in order to express his aggressive behavior in acceptable ways. When he is unsuccessful in this endeavor, he is forced to exhibit his aggressive tendencies in a more inappropriate manner. For instance, Berkowitz always wanted to participate in some heroic deed.[45] Probably because of his low self-esteem and other interpersonal inadequacies, he was prevented from realizing his goal. With this preferred method of expressing aggression blocked, he may have been forced to display his aggressiveness through antisocial behavior.

Thus, it may be that the serial murderer inherits a tendency for aggressive behavior and turns to murder only when more appropriate avenues of venting his aggression are unavailable. Until this inheritable quality is isolated and identified, however, this idea remains theoretical. Much more research is needed before it can be said with any degree of certainty that aggression and violence are passed on. Moreover, even if this were established, investigators would then have to determine whether serial murder occurs because of this inherited trait. At present, any reliance on this explanation is pure speculation.

Increase in the Male Sex Drive

Another cause of serial murder comes from Levin and Fox, who suggest a theory combining both a biological and psychological explanation of an increasing sex drive in men. They assert that serial killers experience difficulty in accepting their decreasing sexual prowess and, as a result, seek out more stimulation in order to achieve sexual arousal. While intercourse remains satisfying to an adolescent, for some older men only sadistic torture is sexually gratifying. The serial murderer pursues this increased need for sexual stimulation to the point of murder.[46] Although this theory seems plausible, there are weaknesses. For example, it ignores the evidence that the serial murderer is emotionally and sexually immature. Since he experiences sex as would an adolescent, he therefore would not need torture and sadistic acts to find gratification. On the contrary, he would be satisfied with normal sexual experiences, thereby contradicting the Levin-Fox theory.

The foregoing contradiction, however, is based upon the psychological sexual development of the serial killer. If this theory were applied purely on a biological analysis, it may be that there is some physiological need that requires sadistic acts in order to satisfy his sexual urges. No biological evidence yet exists, though, to support this view. As a result, any reliance upon this theory to explain serial murder remains premature.

There are obviously a number of biological explanations for aggressive behavior, and many have some merit in helping us better understand violence as well as serial murder. Before any one theory can be relied upon, however, more research must be conducted. The general theories of aggression presented in this chapter need to be further examined and tested specifically with the serial killer in mind. Until this is done, no one biological theory can be looked to with confidence in explaining what motivates serial murder.

Notes

1. Williams at 503; Moyer at 90; Elliot at 57.
2. See Kiloh et al. at 173.
3. Solomon and Davis at 248; Elliot at 57; Norris and Birnes at 173.
4. Stafford-Clark and Taylor at 325; Kiloh et al. at 174.
5. See Wilson and Herrnstein at 201; Bartol at 65 (citing to the following studies: John R. Knott et al., "A Familial Evaluation of the Electroencephalogram of Patients with Primary Behavior Disorder and Psychopathic Personality," *Electroencephalography and Clinical Neurophysiology* 5 [August 1953]: 363–70; S. K. Ehrlich and R. P. Keogh, "The Psychopath in a Mental Institution," *Archives of Neurology and Psychiatry* 76 [July-December 1956]: 286–95; R. G. Arthur and E. B. Cahoon, "A Clinical and Electroencephalographic Survey of the Psycho-

pathic Personality," *American Journal of Psychiatry* 120 [March 1964]: 875–82; Michael Craft, "The Meanings of the Term Psychopath," in *Psychiatric Disorders and Their Assessment*, ed. Michael Craft [Oxford: Pergamon Press, 1966]; and Robert Hare, *Psychopathy: Theory and Research* [New York: John Wiley, 1970]).

6. Kiloh et al. at 172; Bartol at 65.

7. Kiloh et al. at 171 (citing to Denis Hill, "EEG in Episodic Psychotic and Psychopathic Behavior: A Classification of Data," *Electroencephalography and Clinical Neurophysiology* 4 [November 1952]: 419–42); Wolfgang and Weiner at 54. See also Bartol at 65 (citing to Hare, *Psychopathy: Theory and Research*).

8. Kiloh et al. at 172; Bartol at 66.

9. Bartol at 66 (citing to Lee N. Robins, *Deviant Children Grown Up* [Baltimore: Williams and Wilkins, 1966]; T. C. N. Gibbens, D. A. Pond, and D. Stafford-Clark, "A Follow-up Study of Criminal Psychopaths," *British Journal of Delinquency* 5 [September 1955]: 126–36).

10. House of Rep. Hearing at 15.

11. Gibbs and Gibbs at 460; Moyer at 91–92.

12. Epilepsy as used in this context is defined as a recurrent, sudden disorder of cerebral function. See *Taber's Cyclopedic Medical Dictionary* at 608.

13. Gibbs and Gibbs at 461; Bartol at 66; Wilson and Herrnstein at 200.

14. Monroe at 379.

15. Bartol at 66–67, 69.

16. Id. at 69; Solomon and Davis at 257.

17. *Taber's Cyclopedic Medical Dictionary* at 1591; Solomon and Davis at 257; Bartol at 69.

18. Id. at 69–70.

19. Morrison and Minkoff at 343–48; Bartol at 79; Wilson and Herrnstein at 243.

20. Bartol at 77–78.

21. Id. at 70.

22. Michaud and Aynesworth at 63.

23. Kiloh et al. at 28; Restak at 16; Bartol at 198; Norris and Birnes at 177–79.

24. Solomon and Davis at 242; *Taber's Cyclopedic Medical Dictionary* at 1844.

25. MacLean at 300, 296.

26. Restak at 16; Norris and Birnes at 177–78.

27. Restak at 127–28; Gibbs and Gibbs at 234 (citing to Walter Hess, *The Functional Organization of the Diencephalon* [New York: Grune and Stratton, 1957]).

28. Restak at 129, 132.

29. Id. at 133.

30. Wolfgang and Weiner at 54–55; Elliot at 57; Otnow Lewis et al. (1979) at 421; Otnow Lewis et al. (1986) at 840.

31. Otnow Lewis et al. (1986) at 838.

32. Id. at 840.

33. Otnow Lewis et al. (1979) at 422.

34. Bartol at 197.

35. Dorfman at 46; Mawson and Jacobs at 227–30; Lester at 191–92.

36. Goleman (1985) at C1, C8.

37. Id. at C8; Bartol at 197.

38. Wilson and Herrnstein at 69, 100–102; Bartol at 203; Wolfgang and Weiner at 66.

39. Dorfman at 46 (citing to the work of Dr. C. Robert Cloninger of the University of Washington School of Medicine in Seattle).

40. Id.; Wilson and Herrnstein at 96–99.

41. Dorfman at 98, 46.

42. Id. at 46, 98; Wilson and Herrnstein at 100.

43. Schmeck at C3; *Taber's Cyclopedic Medical Dictionary* at 1016–17.

44. Sullivan and Maiken at 235.

45. Abrahamsen (1985) at 31.

46. Levin and Fox at 59.

7 Development of the Serial Murderer

From our examination in Chapter 4, it is apparent that psychiatry has offered many explanations for the cause of serial murder, most of which are inadequate when attempting to discover the complete motivation behind these repeated acts of violence. One theory, however, seems to have gone unexplored and largely unnoticed by the research community. First proposed in 1937 by Dr. Frederic Wertham, this forgotten theory is called the catathymic crisis.[1] As proposed by Wertham, it closely parallels the Freudian/frustration-aggression theory previously discussed in Chapter 5. To a large extent, it is based on the interplay of psychological, sociological, and biological variables that influence human behavior and, as we shall see, holds the key to the mystery of serial murder.

The term *catathymic crisis* rarely, if ever, appears in modern psychiatric journals. Coined by the Swiss psychiatrist, Hans W. Maier, in 1912, the term refers to psychic disorders marked by repetitive actions in which a single topic is the focus. According to Wertham's proposal, a catathymic reaction takes place when a person's strong emotional fears or wishes become fixed in a rutlike fashion on one topic or idea. Through his research work, Wertham discovered in a number of cases a form of catathymic reaction characterized primarily by one feature: the patient acquires the idea that he must perform a violent act either against others or against himself.[2] Furthermore, Wertham pointed out that the individual's idea does not arise from a particular obsession but rather appears as a definite plan, accompanied by an overwhelming urge to carry it out. The violent act usually has some symbolic significance, such as eliminating an ego-threatening or stress-producing relationship. The killer may resist his impulses for some time, but eventually the subject's focus on committing a violent crime takes hold and his thinking becomes rigid and inaccessible to logical reasoning.[3]

Wertham maintained that the clinical position of the catathymic crisis could be visualized as lying within a triangle, the outer points of which are a neurosis, a crisis in personality development, and a psychosis. In addition, he opined that, because of the typical sequence of events consistent with a catathymic crisis, most clinicians are quick to label instances of it as psychopathic behavior, schizophrenia, or compulsive states characterized by strong, irresistible impulses.[4] Indeed, he explained that the diagnosis of catathymic crisis cannot be obtained until an intensive, detailed study of the life history of the patient is conducted.

In formulating his theory, Wertham believed that the catathymic crisis developed in five stages:

1) initial thinking disorders, which follow the original precipitating circumstances;
2) crystallization of a plan, at which time the idea of a violent act emerges into consciousness;
3) extreme tension culminating in the violent crisis in which a brutal act against oneself or others is attempted or carried out;
4) superficial normality beginning with a period of lifting tension and a calmness immediately following the violent act; and
5) insight and recovery with the reestablishment of an inner equilibrium.[5]

In attempting to understand why individuals who exhibit these signs resort to aggressive behavior, Wertham postulated that their violent acts prevent them from developing a more serious mental disorder, such as a neurosis or psychosis, by relieving their mounting tension before it causes a psychological breakdown. He also believed that once stage five is reached the individual understands why he committed the brutal act and thereby extinguishes the urge to carry out any further violence. If the fifth stage is not attained, however, the person suffering from the catathymic crisis returns to the second stage and once again contemplates a violent crime. This subsequent act has a definite symbolic psychological connection to the first, although superficially they may appear very different.[6]

Thus, if the fifth stage of the catathymic crisis is not reached, the process repeats itself. If it is never attained, it is clear that a cyclical pattern of violence emerges, whereby the individual experiences mounting tension released only by committing a brutal crime. This cyclical pattern of the catathymic crisis therefore seems to be the answer to what lies behind the phenomenon of serial murder. As already seen, the serial killer experiences regular periods of increasing tension and restlessness that culminate in murder. Moreover, his life and development parallel remarkably the progressive nature of Wertham's five stages and fits the described pattern. By comparing these stages to the life of the typical serial murderer, it is apparent that his development closely follows the advancing stages of the catathymic crisis.

As described by Wertham, the first stage is one in which initial thinking disorders follow the original precipitating circumstances.[7] With the serial murderer, this step evolves gradually over many years, since his childhood experiences of deprivation or abuse are the original precipitating circumstances. The lack of a stable home environment, and the inconsistent, sometimes violent behavior of his parents, produces substantial detrimental effects. The child never develops any sense of self-worth or self-confidence. He is constantly frustrated by his failure to please his parents, and their inconsistent behavior lends no positive guidance for his development. Despite his usually high IQ, this inability to achieve acceptance or self-worth carries over into his school work and his relationships with others. These frustrations result, on a daily basis, in high levels of stress which the child is ill equipped to deal with because he either was not taught by his parents how to cope, or he has learned from them that violence is the only way to alleviate stress. The outcome of emulating this improper behavior also may be enhanced by an inability of the child's brain structures to manage the incoming stimuli, as a result of a childhood injury or inborn defect. Consequently, the detrimental effects of continued frustration and stress are compounded, thereby causing the child to feel inadequate and helpless.

Despite experiencing these emotions, the child attempts to gain some success and control over his life in small ways, such as trying to please his parents and conforming to their haphazard demands. He also may engage in temper tantrums in order to manipulate others. However, he soon discovers that these efforts to exercise control over his life are futile, and his continuing failures eventually cause him to shun others and withdraw into himself. The result is a child who finds himself alone and helpless, without the love or nurturing that he needs and powerless to remedy his dismal situation.

As a result of these precipitating circumstances, which all occur before adolescence, a form of thinking disorder begins to develop. The child turns to fantasy in an attempt to overcome his failures and to achieve the successes he has been denied in real life. As the FBI study revealed, however, the fantasies are not ones of a wholesome, caring family. Instead, the child focuses on dreaming about gaining respect and importance by exerting control over others.[8]

This focus on fantasized power, rather than on loving family relationships, is probably caused by what the child sees not only in his own home but also in society generally. In his family he recognizes that his parents control his life, and that they may even misuse their power to the point of physical or psychological abuse. The child therefore quickly realizes that the only way to gain control over his own life is to secure that same type of power. In society as well he sees that the most respected individuals are usually those possessing the most power and, as a result, often obtaining what they desire. Thus, the child perceives that the solution to his problems is to achieve and maintain power rather than to work toward attaining a more stable home life.

Once the child turns to his fantasy world, he finds that he is able to achieve that power by creating and orchestrating his own fantasies, in which he can control his make-believe life and those contained in it. Here, he discovers satisfaction in knowing that he can never fail, while, in the real world, he continues to find disappointment and frustration. Consequently, he retreats more and more into his imaginary world of power.[9]

It is clear that, at this point in the serial killer's life, stage one of the catathymic crisis has begun. The fantasy world that he has created, as a result of his detrimental childhood experiences, develops into an obvious thinking disorder. As he grows, his fantasy world eventually becomes a strong part of his existence, since it is only within his fantasies that he finds the power to manipulate others, thereby controlling his own life.[10] It must be remembered, though, that the serial murderer's fantasies are not delusional in nature. He does not hallucinate, nor does he become psychotic. As already seen, overt mental illness is rarely present. Rather, his make-believe world begins in much the same way as do the imaginary playmates that many children create to alleviate loneliness. The difference, however, is that the serial killer's fantasies consume his life, and, instead of abandoning them as he grows older, he develops them into an important part of his day-to-day existence.

This inability to let go of childhood fantasies may be partly due to a maturational retardation within the serial killer because of an impaired brain development. Such a malfunction also would account for his immature emotional development in later life. In addition, the fantasies may persist because he finds more and more comfort and security in them than in the real world. Human nature dictates that the serial murderer is conditioned by this behavior to favor his make-believe world, just as most individuals tend toward activities that provide them with a sense of security.

Once the fantasy world is created, the serial murderer maintains it into adulthood. While in it, close interpersonal relationships become easy, since he can control others and therefore is not vulnerable to rejection. As Abrahamsen relates, this was the case with Berkowitz, who had little incentive to abandon his fantasies for the real world, where rejection was always a frightening possibility. As one of Gacy's employees later revealed, Gacy was always living in a fantasy world. This fantasy existence makes the serial murderer appear to be a shy, quiet loner.[11]

By the time most people are discovering their sexuality, and sharing new experiences with their peers, the serial killer is deeply entrenched in his fantasy world. His initiation into sexual behavior is accomplished not by interaction with others but by concentrating on pornographic literature. From the numerous obscene materials available, he often obtains a distorted view of what normal sexual relationships should be. By remaining in his make-believe world, he satisfies his need for sexual gratification through fantasized sexual conquests, without having to face any chance of rejection. Engaging in various forms of autoerotic behavior, while fantasizing about his sexual victories, eventually becomes so satisfying that the serial killer may continue them even while appearing to maintain a close relationship with a girlfriend, wife, or other sexual partner. If a problem develops with his real relationship, he knows that he can always return to his imaginary world, where he is in complete control of others.[12]

In addition to these advantages of his fantasy existence, the serial murderer also finds that he never has to apologize in his fantasy world because in it he is never wrong. He can obtain what he wants, when he wants it, and does not have to concern himself with how other people feel or how they are affected by his actions. In short, he creates for himself a world in which his needs and desires are paramount, giving absolutely no consideration to others. It is easy to see why he thus gravitates toward this ideal life.

The serial murderer's fantasies soon center upon the use of violence to dominate and control others. Since the parents of many serial murderers used violence as a means of controlling their children's lives, the child perceives this behavior against others as a way of achieving power. Therefore, either a genetic trait for aggressiveness has been passed on from parent to child, or the child learns his violent tendencies by observing his parents. Even if they are not physically abusive, as a child the serial killer still may be encouraged to resort to aggression because of the pervasive nature of violence in society that is portrayed daily on television and in the print media. Violent pornography in particular nurtures within the serial murderer the idea that power and control are achieved through sexual domination. As discussed in Chapter 5, pornographic materials often portray both women and children in submissive roles, while the male is seen as the dominant aggressor. Because of these influencing factors, the serial killer focuses on the use of violence and sexual domination to achieve the power that he otherwise lacks. His fantasies are thus concentrated toward this end.

As the serial killer becomes increasingly enmeshed in his fantasy world, the boundary separating it from reality becomes blurred. This occurs because, pleased with the power and success he has attained in his fantasies, he attempts to transfer these imaginary accomplishments to the real world. As the FBI research team discovered, the serial murderer believes that he can move easily from one world to the other, and that ideas generated in his fantasy existence are viable in reality.[13] Therefore, he presents a facade to the outside world, hoping that he can project to others the image of the powerful man he has dreamed of becoming. He begins to fabricate his accomplishments in order to appear successful, and he uses his intelligence and feigned charm to manipulate those around him. In addition, he might start collecting police paraphernalia, which represent for the serial killer a tremendous source of power. To him, the policeman exercises control over others and indeed is perhaps the most powerful individual in society because he decides who shall remain in public and who shall not. These efforts to transfer his fantasized success and power into the real world, however, are unsuccessful, since the serial murderer continues to fail in most of his endeavors.

The serial killer thus emerges from stage one of the catathymic crisis, in which he has attempted to transfer his fantasized power into reality yet has failed miserably. Stage two soon follows with the realization that a violent act must be carried out in order to turn his fantasy into reality. He discovers that lying and feigned success no longer satisfy his need for power. The gratification formerly experienced in his make-believe world begins to diminish when it becomes more and more apparent that his fantasies are not being fulfilled. His imaginary sexual prowess as well remains nonexistent in the real world, and his efforts to transfer that quality are equally frustrating. He therefore concludes that a violent act is the only way to achieve in reality what he possesses in his fantasy existence. Only through violence can he remedy his constant frustration at not being able to transfer his fantasized power.[14]

The third stage of the catathymic process begins immediately after the second. With the realization that a brutal act must be carried out in order to fulfill his need for power, the serial murderer begins to dwell upon how he will accomplish his task. The feeling to commit this violent act becomes so strong that many serial killers describe it as a "force," a "compulsion," or an "urge" that cannot be controlled.[15] Although he may refrain from this impulse for a time, as Bundy did, his resistance serves only to increase his anxiety about committing the murder.

As the tension builds, the serial murderer begins to look for a victim, many of whom, as we have seen in previous chapters, often resemble one another in physical appearance. Investigators usually postulate that this similarity indicates some symbolic, ritualistic obsession on the part of the killer. However, after realizing that it is his fantasy that orchestrates his actions, it may be that each person selected merely represents his fantasized victim. In his imaginary world, he dominates and controls those he creates. Therefore, he endows these victims with characteristics that he finds attractive or with qualities that he knows he can never possess in reality. Depending upon the individual serial killer, this may be young women with long dark hair or boys with blue eyes. When he transfers his fantasies to the real world, he will thus search for victims who possess these same traits. Only in this way can his fantasy be fulfilled.

In Bundy's case, many believed that he was killing Stephanie over and over again because all of the young women whom he murdered resembled her. Yet, this tells only part of the story. If we realize that, to Bundy, Stephanie was the ideal woman, who was "too good" for him, it is clear that she was the personification of his fantasized victim; she possessed the characteristics that he found to be most attractive. Certainly, then, the rest of his victims would resemble Stephanie, since they all represented, to him, the perfect woman. Thus, he was not only repeatedly killing Stephanie but also his imaginary victim. And this theory applies to Gacy as well, whose fantasized victims were all young boys with certain physical attributes that he found to be appealing.

As the serial killer's tension to commit a violent act upon his ideal victim continues to intensify, he begins to roam the streets with increasing regularity in search of his prey. This incessant hunting provides him with a great deal of excitement and satisfaction, and during this time he dwells upon the crime, anticipating his actions and fantasizing further about the control he will exert over his victim. When the level of anxiety finally reaches unbearable proportions, he succumbs to his urge and attacks his first victim.

As previously discussed, the serial killer's first efforts at murder are often bungled. However, for those few moments during which the assault is occurring, he holds his victim completely in his control and successfully transforms his fantasy into a reality. By relieving his mounting tension and feelings of utter powerlessness, he finally achieves, through violence, the power he has fantasized about for so long. Afterward, he experiences no remorse or regret for his brutal act because, throughout the development of his fantasy, his victim's suffering did not concern him. His own gratification is what is important, and he only knows that he is content with his newfound sense of power.

With the release of tension, the serial murderer finds himself squarely within stage four of the catathymic crisis. The frustration felt because of his perceived powerlessness decreases, and he is calm.[16] He can now direct his efforts at projecting his image of being a successful individual to the outside world without concerning himself with committing another violent act. Furthermore, he can continue to pursue legitimate means of achieving power through business, community service, or political party affiliations, although these activities fail to provide the level of power experienced as a result of his violent attack.

This calmness does not remain with the serial killer for very long, however, since he never reaches stage five of the catathymic process. He does not gain insight into why he has committed a violent act, nor does he realize that it was the result of faulty thinking throughout his life. Rather, he discovers that he enjoys the sense of power experienced through violence. For the first time, he has achieved control in the real world that was otherwise nonexistent for him. He finds this feeling exciting and satisfying, and he dwells upon the crime he has committed.[17] Soon the tension to commit another violent act begins to take hold, as the need to achieve that same sense of power returns. The serial killer then finds himself back in stage two of the catathymic process.

The development of the serial murderer thus parallels quite closely the stages of the catathymic crisis and confirms the observations made by Wertham over fifty years ago. Stage one progresses slowly and is brought on by the many deleterious experiences in the early life of the serial killer. Once stage two is reached the pace of the catathymic process accelerates, and the murderer moves quickly through numbers two, three, and four. Failing to reach stage five, he then returns to stage two and begins the cycle once more. There is, however, an added element to the serial murderer that the catathymic crisis does not take into account. What Wertham could not predict when he formulated his theory is that, when the serial killer starts the catathymic cycle over again, he requires an even more violent act to satisfy his fantasies. Having gained a small sense of power, he then begins to crave more, and, in a subsequent attack, he commits murder. In this way he not only exerts further control over his victim but also increases the amount of power he possesses.[18]

This need for an even greater violent act indicates that the serial killer is engaged in an extreme form of stimulation-seeking activity in order to satisfy his need for power, thereby suggesting a possible malfunction of the brain's reticular activating system. However, as seen in Chapter 6, evidence on this theory is scarce. This need also suggests that the serial killer, because of his immature emotional development, does not know how to control his quest for power. Consequently, his murders become more violent as well as more frequent because of his attempt to gain further power. Eventually he is consumed, or "addicted," by this sense of power. He is not addicted to the act of murder for its own sake nor to any sexual gratification that he may experience from the murders. Rather, he is obsessed with the overwhelming desire for power that these crimes give him, since through them he commands the fate of his victim.

This addiction is also what drives the serial killer further out into the open. By taking more and more chances when he commits his crimes, and by flaunting his acts and taunting law officers, he achieves not only power over his victim but also over the police. He also attains almost total control over the entire community and effectively directs its behavior by the fear he instills through his acts, thereby gaining an incredible sense of satisfaction. In this way, he completely transforms his fantasies into a reality and is finally the powerful individual he has always dreamed of becoming. This may be one reason why he finds peace in prison once he is apprehended. Having completely fulfilled his fantasy, he no longer desires to seek more power. The notoriety and fame that he receives in prison is sufficient to satisfy any remaining need for stimulation. Thus, the tension to commit a violent act subsides, and he is no longer driven to commit murder.

It is apparent, therefore, that the serial murderer's development parallels the pattern in Wertham's catathymic crisis. It allows for variables from the sociological, psychological, and biological fields, thereby providing an accurate description of the development of the serial murderer. Why then has it gone unnoticed among present-day researchers? The answer is found by tracing the theory's subsequent history in the psychiatric field, where one ultimately discovers that the disappearance of Wertham's theory seems due, in part, to the promulgation of other explanations dealing with the motivation for brutal murder. The result was an array of conflicting hypotheses and an almost total obliteration of Wertham's concept.

In 1950, thirteen years after Wertham proposed his catathymic crisis, a report appeared in the *Journal of Clinical Psychopathology* that examined a series of strange murders with no comprehensible motives. Although the bizarreness of these killings indicated schizophrenic behavior, none of the criminals was found to be insane. From this, the authors hypothesized that such murders represented an attempted defense by the ego against the outbreak of a schizophrenic psychosis. They reasoned that aggressive tension intensifies to enormous proportions within some individuals. Since normal ego control mechanisms are not equipped to handle such extreme levels of aggression, the development of a schizophrenic psychosis is possible. To prevent this occurrence, the built-up aggression must be released in some way, and the person suffering from such tension eventually concludes that only an act of tremendous magnitude will accomplish this task. Thus, a violent crime is committed in order to stop the disintegration of the individual's personality.[19]

Proponents of this theory of ego dysfunction used Wertham's catathymic crisis as evidence of the validity of their claims, arguing that the buildup of tension in the murderers they studied paralleled the stages of the catathymic process. Moreover, they explained that, according to Wertham's theory, the sense of relief experienced following a violent act showed that a schizophrenic psychosis was in fact avoided by carrying out the crime. Since the ego is no longer burdened by the built-up aggression, the outbreak of a schizophrenic psychosis no longer threatens the personality. As a result, the individual is safe from severe mental illness and experiences a sense of calmness.

This later theory thus reached the same conclusions as Wertham had about the motivation for seemingly senseless acts of violence such as murder or suicide. Its proponents, however, focused only upon the psychological aspects of Wertham's catathymic crisis for an explanation. Although they stated that the buildup of aggressive tension has its source in childhood frustrations,[20] they went no further in accounting for sociological or biological factors that may influence violent behavior. Their theory of ego dysfunction thus failed to offer an explanation of the development of murder as complete as Wertham's. Nevertheless, it formed the basis of a subsequent report on violence.

In 1956 the influential Menninger Clinic in Topeka, Kansas, published a report on aggression describing a disorder that was marked by outbursts of explosive violence, preceded by mounting emotional tension, and followed by periods of relief. Subsequent to the relief, some individuals experienced a re-accumulation of anxiety. The authors of this report termed this disorder *episodic dyscontrol* and based their explanation of this type of violent behavior on the earlier idea that the ego performs a protective function against mental breakdown. They noted that when tensions become too great within an individual, the ego "gives way," allowing some of the aggressive impulses to escape.[21] In other words, the ego "ruptures" in order to relieve the overwhelming tension that, if unreleased, would cause a serious disintegration in a person's mental health.

The Menninger report then went on to divide individuals with this disorder into two groups: those showing organized and consciously rationalized behavior, and those manifesting disorganized aggressive behavior that the ego does not even attempt to justify or explain. In the organized group, which includes sociopaths and psychopaths, disturbances of consciousness are infrequent, and the killer usually rationalizes his behavior. Those in this category often depart from the rules of society and from using sound judgment. Individuals in the disorganized group usually undergo an obvious break with reality, as evidenced by the chaotic nature of their crimes, and they may experience a loss of consciousness or memory of their acts. The authors of this report, in mentioning Wertham's theory only briefly, determined that instances of the catathymic crisis should be placed within this latter group.[22]

Wertham's basic theory of catathymic crisis, then, was included in the Menninger report but under the broader concept of episodic dyscontrol. This marked not only a change in nomenclature but also a shift to a purely psychological basis for explaining violent behavior. Rather than discussing the sociological causes of the mounting tension, the report focused upon the rupturing of the ego. Indeed, it made no mention at all of the factors contributing to this ego breakdown. Accordingly, it, too, failed to give as complete an explanation for murder as did Wertham's theory. Moreover, the Menninger report maintained that some catathymic crises are characterized by a complete break with reality. How this conclusion was reached is far from clear, for nowhere did Wertham assert such a proposal. Yet the report classified instances of the catathymic crisis squarely within the disorganized group of offenders. Therefore, this misclassification of Wertham's theory has served only to cloud the original hypothesis and distort its actual meaning.

In 1960, not long after the promulgation of the episodic dyscontrol theory, a paper published in the *American Journal of Psychiatry* attempted to illustrate the concept.[23] In this report, researchers studied four one-time murderers who seemed to share many common characteristics; they were rational, coherent, and controlled, yet their homicidal acts were bizarre and apparently senseless. In comparing the murders committed by these men, it was noted that there were no accompanying crimes, such as burglary or robbery, nor did any of the killers appear to gain economically or politically from their acts. Each killer's victim was unknown to him, and the impromptu methods of murder used were often bare hands or whatever else was immediately available. In each case the attacks were unnecessarily brutal and lasted long after the victim's death.[24]

When the backgrounds of these murderers were examined, numerous striking similarities also were discovered. Each man had experienced a long history of erratic control over his aggressive impulses and frequently had been involved in fights. All four saw themselves as physically inferior, weak, and inadequate, and each had a severe degree of sexual inhibition. There was also evidence of periods of altered, or trancelike, states of consciousness, often in connection with their outbursts of violence. Furthermore, each killer reported that during his childhood he had experienced extreme parental abuse and emotional deprivation, which were taken for granted as natural occurrences in life.

Moreover, they learned from their parents that violence is often associated with the sexual behavior of adults.[25]

In addition to the similarities found in the murderers' backgrounds, researchers discovered, in their clinical examinations of these men, a number of common characteristics. All four had a disturbance of impulse control, exhibiting an "all-or-nothing" pattern of functioning. Once their self-control began to weaken, they were almost completely overwhelmed by emotion, morbid fantasies, and a proneness to immediate, unreflective response, whereby they would take action without first thinking about the consequences. There were manifestations in each of a bizarre and violent fantasy life (characterized by thoughts of killing, mutilating, or destroying others), with a blurring of the boundaries between fantasy and reality. In addition, these criminals' relationships with others were often of a shallow, cold nature, lending a quality of loneliness and isolation to their lives. Finally, researchers observed that guilt, depression, and remorse were strikingly absent from these murderers' personalities. From these findings, they therefore concluded that, when apparently senseless murders occur, they are the result of a period of increasing tension within the killer, who then chooses a victim simply because that individual fits into his "unconscious conflicts." These types of criminals are "murder-prone" because they either possess an excessive amount of aggressive energy, or they suffer from an unstable ego defense system that periodically allows the expression of violent impulses.[26]

This report in the *American Journal of Psychiatry* served to illustrate the concepts in the episodic dyscontrol theory. However, it described as well the stages of Wertham's catathymic crisis. By discussing the fantasy life of a murderer, his mounting tension, and finally his act of a violent crime, the report was obviously describing incidences of the catathymic process. It is just as clear that the behavior and characteristics of the murderers studied in this survey also closely resemble those of the present-day serial murderer. One would assume, therefore, that the authors would recognize that the episodic dyscontrol theory and the catathymic crisis describe essentially the same behavior. On the contrary, the only reference to Wertham in this report served to distinguish occurrences of the catathymic process from the murders discussed. This study therefore maintained that the senseless acts committed against relatively unknown persons were different from catathymic crisis murders, asserting that the latter type of crime only arises out of protracted but conflictual relationships, such as with a wife, child, or parent.[27]

Thus, without further explanation, Wertham's theory was relegated to just those murderous acts involving family members, thereby completely excluding those against strangers. How this distinction was reached is not discussed in the report. It is clear, however, that this was an improper distinction, since one of Wertham's own examples of the catathymic crisis—the murders committed by Robert Irwin—involved three people: two of whom he knew very casually while the third was a stranger. Yet, because this distinction was made, the catathymic crisis theory was disregarded as an explanation of the murders against strangers described in the report.

Also in 1960, Dr. Manfred Guttmacher, writing in his book *The Mind of the Murderer*, discussed episodic dyscontrol as well as the catathymic crisis. After reviewing Wertham's 1937 proposal, as well as the 1950, 1956, and 1960 studies, he asserted that the murderous activity exhibited by those killers who showed no signs of mental illness and who acted suddenly and violently without motive was the result of an intense, repressed hostility together with a defective ego with weak, brittle defenses. However, he disagreed with the proposition that these acts represented an attempted defense against the outbreak of a schizophrenic psychosis. In rebutting this theory, Guttmacher argued that psychological defense mechanisms are rarely used by an individual only once in his lifetime; rather, they are more likely to be habitual in nature and used repeatedly over time.[28] By stressing this, however, Guttmacher ignored the fact that catathymic crisis murders, as well as incidences of episodic dyscontrol, can recur and are not always confined to one instance of violence. Thus, the basis for his disagreement is apparently unsound.

In formulating his own theory, Guttmacher pointed out that the nature of the crimes committed by those suffering from episodic dyscontrol or catathymic crisis strongly suggests a psychotic act, yet, when these types of killers are examined, no evidence of psychosis is discovered. He therefore concluded that the murders committed by such individuals were all instances of short-lived psychic decompensation due to external or interpsychic stress.[29] In other words, he postulated that the buildup of tension, together with a weak ego control, resulted in a temporarily psychotic individual. Thus, Guttmacher offered a purely psychological explanation for the kinds of murders studied by Wertham. This alternative only served to obscure further the meaning of Wertham's original theory since it, too, failed to account for the many other factors contributing to these senseless, brutal, and motiveless acts committed by seemingly normal individuals.

In subsequent years, several researchers have studied the occurrence of violent outbursts in men.[30] Discovering the same personal, familial, and clinical characteristics in their subjects as their predecessors had, they chose to label the violent crimes of their subjects as incidents of episodic dyscontrol. In addition, others describing exactly the same behavioral patterns coined new diagnostic terms for their subjects, such as *epileptoid personality, aggressive personality,* and *explosive personality.*[31] Rarely, if ever, was the catathymic crisis mentioned.

This disappearance of Wertham's theory was remedied in 1981 when a group of researchers presented an updated and somewhat modified version. They postulated that a catathymic crisis can arise out of any ego-threatening relationship that causes a feeling of sexual inadequacy, helplessness and confusion, and a transfer of hostile emotions from one subject to a symbolic victim. The conflict experienced from these relationships leads to unbearable tension, which is then released by committing a violent act. This revised version considered the catathymic crisis to be a psychodynamic process rather than a diagnostic entity, as Wertham had proposed, and described only three stages of development—the incubation, violent act, and relief stages—rather than the original five.[32]

During the incubation period the individual is obsessed with his future victim and experiences depression or distorted thinking. Initial thoughts of suicide intermingle with fantasies of murder, which ultimately dominate in the killer's mind. He may struggle with his urgent need to commit violence, and may even seek out help by telling others, but his warnings are often misunderstood or ignored. Although his criminal act may appear preplanned, he perceives this seeming premeditation as merely a thought that is divorced from action.[33]

In addition, this updated version divided the disorder into two groups: acute catathymic process and chronic catathymic process. In the former category, the violent act is triggered by some sudden overwhelming emotion that is connected to an idea of symbolic significance; the incubation period is very short, perhaps several seconds; there is a lessening of emotions after the act; the victim is usually a stranger; and the killer's memory of the event is poor. With the chronic catathymic process, the violent act is brought on by a buildup of tension, a sense of frustration, depression, and helplessness; the incubation period can be any-where from several days to one year; there is a feeling of relief following the event; the victim is usually a family member or someone sharing a close relationship with the killer; and a memory of the act is preserved.[34] Although the victims are usu-ally close relations, the accumulation of tension caused by a sense of helplessness and confusion also can be released upon a stranger or in an explosive mass murder.[35] Of the two types, the chronic form of the catathymic process most closely resembles Wertham's original theory.

With the advent of this new version of the catathymic crisis, this theory was reestablished as an explanation for violent out-bursts. Modern proponents as well dispelled the notion that incidences of catathymic violence occur only against close rela-tions or family members. It was thus once more recognized that brutal acts against strangers can be the result of a catathymic crisis. While Wertham's theory was being revised, however, other researchers were expanding upon the episodic dyscontrol theory, which by 1981 was well established. At that time, it was defined as an abrupt, single act or short series of acts that are not characteristic of the life-style of the individual. These acts share a common purpose and provide the offender relief from tension, or at least an immediate gratification of a specific need, and they usually represent an impulsive expression of primitive fear-rage emotions, whereby the individual's control mechanisms, for-merly called the ego, are overcome. Violence then occurs either when excessively strong urges overwhelm normal control mechanisms, or when regular impulses are uncontrolled by weak or deficient inhibitory mechanisms.[36]

In addition, two distinct types of dyscontrol behaviors were recognized: primary and secondary. In instances of primary dyscontrol the individual seeks immediate gratification as a reaction to certain environmental stimuli without ever considering any possible alternatives involving delay. This category therefore includes those individuals whose acts are committed during a seizure or performed on instinct, with little or no regard for the consequences. With secondary dyscontrol, there is either a conscious or unconscious premeditation that precedes the violent action and is thought to indicate an ambivalent, vacillating attitude on the part of the offender regarding his decision either to give in to or refrain from acting on his impulses.[37] Accordingly, this newer version of episodic dyscontrol classifies offenders based upon how immediate their reaction is to stressful stimuli. An instantaneous reaction indicates primary dyscontrol, while a delayed response signifies secondary dyscontrol.

Furthermore, researchers also began to recognize by 1981 that occurrences of episodic dyscontrol are not solely attributable to psychological processes. It therefore was acknowledged that such violent behavior may be due in part to a maturational lag in the development of the nervous system or to some form of temporal lobe epilepsy. This concession came as a response to the increasing evidence showing that brain dysfunction, as indicated by EEG readings, is associated with explosive, fearful, and aggressive actions. Moreover, the impact of learned behavior also was realized as an important factor in explaining episodic dyscontrol.[38] These admissions marked an expansion of the original episodic dyscontrol theory, which initially had focused almost entirely upon psychiatric concepts. It as well suggested a shift back toward Wertham's original catathymic crisis, which allowed for the examination of sociological, biological, and psychological factors.

It seems that the catathymic crisis and episodic dyscontrol theories thus developed simultaneously into two independent theories, although each described substantially the same behavior. Since most researchers relied upon the episodic dyscontrol theory, and many in fact still do so even today, this is in all likelihood why Wertham's catathymic process was overlooked for so long.[39] Finally, however, these two hypotheses were brought together in the third edition of the *Diagnostic and Statistical*

Manual of Mental Disorders (DSM-III). When it was published in 1981, it did not adopt either the term *catathymic crisis* or *episodic dyscontrol* as an official diagnostic label. Proponents of the latter theory maintain that the concept of the dyscontrol syndrome was used in the DSM-III as the diagnostic criteria to explain explosive disorders. They assert that the intermittent explosive disorder described in the DSM-III mirrors episodic dyscontrol behavior and, in fact, is based upon published accounts of the dyscontrol syndrome.[40] Furthermore, they argue that psychiatry simply chose to abandon the term *episodic dyscontrol* and adopt the term *explosive disorder* to describe this type of violent behavior.

The DSM-III, in describing explosive disorders, explains that there are two types: the isolated explosive disorder and the intermittent explosive disorder.[41] Both are characterized by actions that exceed the social norm, an increasing sense of emotional discomfort that builds prior to the commission of the deed, and the act itself is often ego-syntonic, whereby the offender experiences pleasure, gratification, sexual excitement, or release from tension at the time of the crime.[42]

The isolated explosive disorder consists of a single, discrete episode in which an individual's failure to resist an impulse leads to a single, violent, externally directed act that has a catastrophic impact on others. Prior to the episode, there are no signs of generalized impulsivity or aggressiveness; however, the degree of aggression expressed during the incident is grossly out of proportion to any precipitating psychosocial stressors. When an individual exhibits several distinct episodes of isolated explosive behavior, the diagnosis is then changed to intermittent explosive disorder. Just as with the former disorder, the individual's behavior is entirely out of proportion to any precipitating factors, and there is an absence of generalized impulsivity or aggression between each act.[43]

During an aggressive occurrence of an explosive disorder, the individual may experience subtle changes in the senses, such as hypersensitivity to loud noises or bright lights, and there may be partial amnesia after the act is completed. The offender's behavior is usually a surprise to those who know him, and the person himself may be startled by his own actions. In addition, the individual sometimes explains that the events resulted from a compelling force beyond his control. After the attack, the person may feel genuine regret for the consequences of his actions as well as concern for his inability to control his aggressive impulses.[44]

The authors of the *DSM*-III noted that explosive disorders, more common in males than in females, may begin at any age but usually have their onset while the individual is in his twenties or thirties. It is also believed that any toxic substance, such as alcohol, that may lower the threshold for violent outbursts, as well as conditions conducive to brain dysfunction, such as perinatal trauma, infantile seizures, head injuries, or encephalitis, may predispose a person to this disorder. Furthermore, nonspecific brain abnormalities or minor neurological signs thought to reflect subcortical or limbic system dysfunction may be factors.[45]

Once promulgated, the episodic dyscontrol theory aligned itself to the explosive disorders quite rapidly. This was a wholly proper alliance, since both describe essentially the same condition. It is apparent, however, that the explosive disorders also closely parallel the catathymic crisis. Indeed, the authors of the *DSM*-III recognized as much when, in describing isolated explosive behavior, they noted that this disorder was referred to in the past as "catathymic crisis."[46] Therefore, it was finally realized by the psychiatric community that the catathymic process and the episodic dyscontrol theory both describe the same phenomenon.

Although the explosive disorders discussed in the *DSM*-III substantially describe what Wertham observed in his catathymic crisis theory, they provide an inadequate analysis when examining the reasons for the motivation behind serial murder. The major flaw, and indeed the strongest criticism of the entire *DSM*-III, is that it describes only the outward symptoms of an individual who exhibits explosive behavior. The authors do not discuss any developmental factors leading up to the eventual aggressive act, nor do they indicate the cause of the need for violence. Thus, any attempt to utilize these disorders to explain the phenomenon of serial murder is severely limited.

In addition, the *DSM*-III used the concept of catathymic crisis only to describe the type of murderer who explodes in a single episode of extreme violence. This ignores the fact that the catathymic process is capable of repetition, whereby an individual commits a series of violent acts. Moreover, the serial killer does not show any evidence of a change in the senses during the murder, nor does he experience regret afterward. Because these are characteristics of someone suffering from an explosive disorder, this behavior therefore does not describe the serial killer.

More importantly, however, the entire classification of explosive disorders has come under substantial criticism by the psychiatric community. As a result of the high potential for misdiagnosis based upon a single act of aggression, the revised edition of the *DSM-III* (*DSM-III-R*), published in 1987, completely omits isolated explosive disorder as a diagnostic label. Although intermittent explosive disorder has been retained, the authors warn that its validity as a psychiatric disorder is questionable.[47] Accordingly, this present-day description of the behavior originally described by Wertham is clearly inadequate, and any reliance upon explosive disorders to explain serial murder is certainly misplaced.

In summary, then, it is evident from tracing the history of the catathymic crisis that Wertham's theory, for the most part, was ignored by researchers in subsequent years. It is clear, however, that the most complete and accurate description of the development of the serial murderer comes from following the five stages of the catathymic process. Modern attempts to explain the phenomenon simply fall short and lack the thoroughness of Wertham's original theory. Even the modified version fails to explain adequately the serial killer's motivation by restricting his development to only three stages and limiting the incubation period to a maximum of one year. With the serial murderer, it is obvious that the incubation period is quite prolonged, starting with childhood fantasies and continuing into adult life. In addition, although the serial killer never reaches stage five, his development parallels the original theory's detailed stages rather than the generalized stages contained in the modern version. It is therefore apparent that the original catathymic crisis theory is more appropriate when describing serial murder and should be utilized instead of the modern theories that have been proposed. Only in this way can a better understanding of the serial murderer's development and motivation be obtained.

Notes

1. Wertham (1937) at 974.
2. *Dorland's Illustrated Medical Dictionary* at 230. See also Wertham (1937) at 975–76.
3. Wertham (1937) at 976; Wertham (1941) at 225; Wertham (1966) at 238.
4. Wertham (1937) at 976.
5. Wertham (1941) at 226–27; Wertham (1949) at 179.
6. Wertham (1937) at 978; Wertham (1941) at 230, 255–56; Wertham (1949) at 179.
7. Wertham (1949) at 179.
8. Burgess et al. at 257; FBI-August 1985 at 4; Finkelhor at 362.
9. Burgess et al. at 264–65.
10. Id. at 263.
11. Abrahamsen (1985) at 168; Sullivan and Maiken at 64.
12. Ressler et al. (1986b) at 283.
13. FBI-August 1985 at 9.
14. Norris and Birnes at 211.
15. Cheney at 139–40; Egger at 268; Leyton at 49, 126, 136; Kendall at 174.
16. Ressler et al. (1986b) at 284.
17. Egger at 30; Levin and Fox at 68; Ressler et al. (1986b) at 284.
18. Egger at 30, 304; Levin and Fox at 72.
19. Reichard and Tillman at 149–51.
20. Id. at 149.
21. Menninger and Mayman at 153, 156.
22. Id. at 157, 163.
23. Satten et al. at 48.
24. Id. at 49.
25. Id. at 49–50.
26. Id. at 50–52.
27. Id. at 52.
28. Guttmacher at 56–57, 62–63.
29. Id. at 63.
30. Bach-y-Rita et al. at 49.
31. Pasternack at 45–69; Morrison and Minkoff at 343–48; Monopolis and Lion at 1200–1202.
32. Revitch and Schlesinger at 127–50, 128, 136.
33. Id. at 136–37.
34. Id. at 129.
35. Id. at 137, 145.
36. Monroe at 371–72, 375.
37. Id. at 374.
38. Id. at 378–81.
39. Norris and Birnes at 19, 186.
40. Monroe at 385.
41. *Diagnostic and Statistical Manual of Mental Disorders*, 3d ed. at 295–98 (hereafter *DSM*-III).
42. Ginsberg at 1099.
43. *DSM*-III at 298, 297.
44. Id. at 296.

45. Id.
46. Id. at 297; Campion et al. at 316.
47. *DSM*-III-R at 427, 321.

8 Suggestions for Preventing Future Serial Murder

It is evident that the serial murderer poses a unique problem for both law enforcement and society. The nature of the crime itself, as well as the inability of police personnel to respond effectively, results in a frustrating and inefficient attempt to prevent serial murder. With an increased knowledge and understanding of the murderer, however, advances can be achieved. By recognizing what causes serial murder, law enforcement authorities particularly, and society as a whole, can make great strides in preventing the development of future serial killers.

Society's first step toward this effort is to lend support to the victims of child abuse, for one of the most serious precipitating factors leading to the development of serial murderers is their childhood abuse and neglect. The detrimental future impact on their personality from this harsh treatment is quite severe. Prior to the early 1960s the abuse of children was scarcely even considered by the general public, and, in fact, it was not seen as a concern at all.[1] Since that time, however, societal awareness of child abuse and neglect has grown considerably. Citizens, private organizations, and governmental agencies are all now acutely sensitive to the plight of the abused child and are lending their overwhelming support.

Before any abused children can receive outside assistance, someone must first recognize that they are being mistreated. This can be a difficult task, since the effects of abuse can vary and are sometimes not readily apparent. If there are no obvious bruises or other physical signs, the mistreatment can go undetected. Although doctors and hospital emergency-room personnel are now required by law to report cases of suspected child abuse, they can do so only if the parent seeks medical treatment for his child. If none is sought, however, the abuse remains undetected, thereby leaving the child with no hope for assistance.

These difficulties substantially diminish once the child begins to attend school, where he not only has daily contact with responsible adults, but he also interacts with other children. Eventually, he may confide in someone and reveal his torment. Even if he does not speak up, however, school officials still play an important role in the detection of abuse and neglect, since certain behavioral signs exhibited by children, including undue hostility, overaggressiveness or overpassivity and withdrawal, isolation from others, fear of parents, frequent daydreaming, and short attention span, are often indicators of possible maltreatment. Although experts caution that these signs do not always mean that abuse is present, they may suggest problems in the child's development that should be explored.[2] By knowing what to look for in a child's behavior, educators therefore can contribute greatly to the early detection of abuse.

Once the victim of child abuse or neglect is identified, society can respond in various ways. Many researchers find that children, especially very young ones, are highly susceptible to the environmental influences that surround them. Although this makes them more vulnerable to abuse and neglect, it also makes them more receptive to therapeutic efforts.[3] Accordingly, over the last twenty-five years numerous treatment, counseling, and educational programs have been developed to assist the victims of abuse and neglect. Thus, society is coming to the aid of these innocent children.

Simply treating the child, however, is not enough to remedy the problem. To do so merely attacks the symptom and not the cause of child abuse. Instead, experts now agree that the entire family must be involved in the treatment process if the abused and neglected child is to be helped at all. One successful method is the use of family counseling, in both individual and group sessions.[4] In this way, each person learns to cope with and overcome his own guilt, fear, and anxiety, while learning to understand the feelings of other family members, perhaps for the first time.

For the abused child, these counseling sessions address important developmental problems such as the lack of trust in adults and in interpersonal relationships, the need for nurturance, poor self-esteem and judgment, inability to express emotions, and lack of confidence in his own abilities.[5] The child also has the opportunity to discuss and overcome his feelings of worthlessness and helplessness, thereby giving him a sense of control and direction in his life. In this way, family counseling may head off a critical stage in the development of the serial murderer by preventing the onset of a strong fantasy life. In addition, through counseling, the abusive parent can learn to express his or her frustration in productive ways rather than through violence and therefore decrease the actual abuse inflicted upon the child. These sessions also can expose parents to educational and supportive programs aimed at enhancing their own self-esteem and lowering their sometimes unrealistic expectations for the child.[6] As a result, the parent is better able to cope with daily problems and is less abusive.

Another form of support for abusive families is found in such efforts as the Parents and Children Together (PACT) project and the Lay Home Visitor Program,[7] which both provide aid in the form of better housing, child care, and nutritional education. In so doing, they offer a form of assistance that in turn alleviates the stress of daily living for many families and fosters a more comfortable, nurturing atmosphere within the abusive home. Programs such as these can be of critical importance in the fight against serial murder, since the serial killer's life, as we have seen, lacks a loving and caring environment.

There are many other community organizations that aid the abusive family and particularly the abusive parent. One of the best known is Parents Anonymous, which gives parents a place to meet and discuss their problems without the fear of reprisal or persecution.[8] Similar organizations include Parents United, the Nurturing Program, the Milwaukee Project, Family Focus, the Michigan Drop-in Center, the Hugs 'n' Kids program, the Systematic Training for Effective Parenting (STEP) program, and the Minnesota Early Learning Design (MELD) program.[9] All of these offer therapeutic group sessions, peer counseling, professional counseling, and various educational programs designed to teach proper parenting techniques. Clearly, their efforts go a long way in preventing future child abuse.

Thus, there are a number of community-based measures designed to aid the abusive family. In many cases the abuse can be stopped and families can be reunited through these various societal efforts. The treatment of emotionally, physically, or sexually abused and neglected children, however, is still in its infancy. Indeed, at least 10 percent of all abusive families are completely unresponsive to attempts at treatment. When this occurs, society is left with no other choice but to remove the child from his home and place him in foster care.[10] However, this alternative can be a confusing and unsettling experience for the child, who may feel like an outcast in his new surroundings. Ultimately, this situation may intensify his feelings about being unwanted and unloved by his own family, as well as destroy any relationship he might have formerly enjoyed with his natural parents. Moreover, according to one report, the risk of maltreatment by a foster parent is over three times greater than the risk of abuse by a natural parent.[11] It is therefore not surprising to find that foster care placement is usually reserved for only the most severe cases of abuse or neglect and used only when there is no other solution.[12]

Besides community efforts, the problem of child abuse is being addressed at the national level as well. In 1974 the Federal Child Abuse Act was passed, establishing a National Center on Child Abuse and Neglect. Ten years later the U.S. Justice Department created the National Center for Missing and Exploited Children, which operates twenty-four hours per day and maintains a toll-free number to report incidences of child abuse. Also in 1984 the U.S. attorney general formed a task force to address family violence and conducted hearings on the subject throughout the country. In addition, a presidential commission, established in 1985, issued its final report in 1987 giving a number of recommendations to the public and private sectors on the problems of child abuse and exploitation. Finally, a number of private organizations have been formed that deal with the welfare of children, including the National Committee for Prevention of Child Abuse, the American Humane Association's Children's Division, and the National Child Abuse Coalition.[13]

The efforts of these local and national organizations indicate that society has finally begun to accept its responsibility in caring for its younger members. No longer is the mistreatment of children viewed solely as a matter to be dealt with by the family alone. Rather, support services and self-help groups are now firmly in place and contribute immensely to the reduction of child abuse and neglect. What this means in the fight against serial murder is that, if society can eliminate or at least reduce the incidence of child abuse, it will certainly decrease the number of potential serial killers. By ensuring a loving, nurturing homelife for children, society will be helping to prevent the initial stage of a tragic sequence of events that can culminate in the development of multiple murderers. Accordingly, child abuse programs should be supported and encouraged whenever possible.

Although eliminating child abuse is apparently the ideal way to deter serial murder, this approach does not address the problem of the abused child who is now an adult. As we have seen, the effects of being mistreated and neglected have a long-standing impact on behavior well into adulthood and, indeed, are often contributing factors toward the strong motivational forces behind the serial killer's acts. Yet the programs designed to alleviate the stress of child abuse do not follow him into adulthood. Fortunately, society has begun to recognize the plight of these individuals, and, in recent years, support groups have emerged that deal specifically with the problems facing the "grown-up abused child." During group sessions, these adults are encouraged to discuss the abuse that was inflicted upon them and how it affected them, both as children and later as adults. This approach breaks down feelings of isolation; provides a safe and supportive environment for the expression of emotions; offers a consistent, predictable response by others; fosters trust in people and in the participants themselves; encourages members to take greater control of their lives; and promotes better interpersonal relationships. More importantly, it leads to in-depth revelations about inner feelings and fantasies, thereby allowing group members to work through their emotions. In this way, they are able to gain control over their feelings and find a sense of freedom and self-confidence.[14]

For the potential serial murderer, this approach offers significant hope. The once-abused child, who entertains violent and sadistic fantasies as an adult, now has assistance and support. He can discuss his fantasies and emotions with people who understand his pain and can offer comfort. If this individual is encouraged to use the group as an outlet for his fantasies, he is much less likely to carry them out, thereby helping to forestall the onset of serial murder. Therefore, through this group process the potential killer learns to confront and then control his fantasies, which in turn prevents his imaginary world from overpowering him and directing his behavior. In this way, actual murder may never occur at all, and this is exactly the outcome that society seeks in its fight against serial murder.

There are, however, several problems with this approach to combating serial murder. The first is that this type of group therapy is entirely self-motivated, and, as such, the potential killer must want to be helped. He must take the initiative and seek out the group for assistance, or he cannot benefit from the process. Second, the serial killer may not even recognize that part of his adult problems result from his childhood deprivation. Without realizing this, he certainly will not seek out a group designed to deal with the problems of grown-up abused children. Third, even if he does begin group sessions, he may become discouraged and drop out, finding that the introspection and revelation required for participation are simply too painful. Indeed, this is a common problem with many forms of personal therapy. Finally, adults who were abused as children are quite often unable or unwilling to give up their well-established defense mechanisms of withdrawn emotions, aversion to intimate relationships, and distrust of others, thereby making a productive group process almost impossible.[15]

These difficulties aside, however, it is clear that therapy groups designed to confront the problems experienced by grown-up abused children are extremely worthwhile. For the first time, abused children are receiving help and encouragement even after they become adults. By supporting these efforts, society is not only helping a forgotten portion of its populace, but it is also addressing the problems of the potential serial murderer. By allowing the potential killer to reveal and explore his fantasies, society is thus effectively helping to prevent serial murder. Accordingly, these group sessions should be established in every community.

Having explored what society can do to deter serial murder from ever starting, we turn next to what can be done once a serial killer begins his murderous spree. Traditionally, the success rate for apprehending these criminals has been quite low. In fact, the serial killer is usually discovered purely by coincidence and not by any established investigative procedure. Although his repeated acts are sometimes committed in broad daylight, he evades detection and avoids capture because of the scarcity of physical evidence left at the scene.[16] This, along with his intelligence and mobility, may render him virtually invisible to police for many years.

Complicating this already difficult task are the procedures used by many police agencies in handling missing persons. Quite often when someone is reported missing, local authorities do nothing for the first twenty-four to forty-eight hours. They simply consider it a routine runaway case and wait to see if the person returns home. These first few hours, however, are the most critical period in a homicide case. Indeed, law enforcement officers generally agree that, if a suspect is not located within the first two or three days, the chances of ever finding him decrease substantially. Yet this delay in the investigation of missing persons persists, even when parents adamantly oppose the notion that their child has run away.[17] Therefore, police departments around the country must abandon the twenty-four to forty-eight-hour waiting period, during which critical moments may slip by, resulting in disastrous consequences. It is clear from the cases that we have examined that any reduction in the amount of time the serial killer has to commit his crime and escape will surely aid in his capture.

Perhaps the most inexcusable and tragic practice of many law enforcement agencies is their unwillingness to share information. In many serial murder investigations, local and state police departments refuse to cooperate with other local, state, and federal agencies participating in the same investigation. Petty jealousies and intense rivalries between departments often run high, closing off cooperative measures and making an effective investigation all but impossible.[18] Even within individual police departments, the lack of communication is astonishing. As seen with the Chicago police, many times the separate divisions of a department never share the information they obtain. As a result, the obvious links between the serial killer and his victims often go unnoticed. Indeed, this is what allowed Gacy to continue his murderous acts.

Other examples of this failure to communicate are readily apparent. During the Boston Strangler investigation, police searched their computer files for possible suspects, but they only checked the files of known sex offenders. Since DeSalvo's name was entered in the breaking-and-entering files, his name never came up. In the search for the Hillside Strangler, three police agencies joined forces at a central location and entered all of their information on a computer. Although a commendable effort, it proved of little value, since the computer could not cross-reference the data entered by each of the three agencies.[19] Thus, common traits found in the murders by each separate agency were never compared.

In addition, the FBI, with its wide network of resources, usually cannot participate in the investigation of a murder unless assistance is requested by the local agencies. Since the vast majority of murders committed in the United States are not federal crimes, the FBI lacks the jurisdiction to pursue the murderer, even when his crimes are committed in several states.[20] Accordingly, it cannot investigate or prosecute serial murderers on its own initiative; rather, it first must be invited to do so by local authorities. Tragically, this process usually leaves the federal resources untapped during the search for the killer.

Recognizing these deficiencies in their investigative practices, law enforcement personnel across the country are suggesting better, more efficient ways of combating serial murder through conferences, information clearinghouses, task forces, investigative consultant teams, and psychological profiling. The conferences, for example, are designed to distribute information to a variety of police officers on the topic of serial murderers. There are generally two types of conferences: those dealing with numerous unsolved murders and those concerned with the identification and capture of a specific serial murderer. Both have proven effective in the investigation of serial killings. Likewise, the information clearinghouses also allow for the dissemination of information among police agencies. When created, they act as central repositories for all information concerning any unsolved murders that might be linked to a known or unknown serial murderer. Clearinghouses thus provide information to all jurisdictions involved in the case and can coordinate data among them.[21] In this way, patterns of behavior can be established, and unsolved homicides can be examined to determine if they are related.

These law enforcement efforts mark a substantial step forward in the fight against the serial killer. Since they function only through the cooperation of many different police agencies, the jealousies, competitiveness, and traditional notions of isolationism that formerly characterized agency relations are set aside. Each reports to and exchanges information with other law enforcement departments, thereby keeping open the lines of communication. These methods are also valuable since they allow for the comparison of many homicides from several states.[22] Only in this way can the highly mobile serial murderer be traced and then identified. This process, however, can be long and tedious, especially when there are large numbers of homicides to analyze from all across the country. In addition, coordinating a meeting time and place for police officers from different states can be an arduous task. As we shall see later in this chapter, a much more efficient method of comparing cases state to state has been established through the use of a centralized computer system.

The formation of a task force, in which representatives from each jurisdiction or agency involved in solving a serial murder join together as a single investigative unit, also has been a successful practice. This procedure eliminates duplication of effort and ensures that any evidence that is uncovered is handled properly.[23] In this way, the task force draws the resources of several police agencies into one centralized location where a strong, concerted attempt at resolving the crimes can be mounted.

Still another method is the investigative consultant team. First introduced in the Atlanta child killings, it consists of a number of detectives chosen from various police departments throughout the country because of their expertise in handling multiple murder cases. These individuals work closely with local investigators, making recommendations and sharing any insight they may have as a result of their experience. Team members do not take over the investigation but rather offer a "second opinion" to local police detectives.[24]

Finally, the utilization of a psychological profile is one more police procedure now in practice to combat serial murder.[25] To formulate this profile, a painstaking analysis is conducted, noting patterns that appear in each crime, characteristics of the victims, and methods used by the killer. Every aspect of the murder is scrutinized in detail, since the personality of the serial killer is often reflected in the crime scenes he leaves behind. By studying the results, the profiler hopes to identify and list the characteristics that the killer is likely to possess. Armed with this information, police can narrow the class of potential suspects by concentrating on those individuals who possess the traits enumerated in the profile.[26]

Although these psychological profiles can be helpful in the investigation of serial murder, their use has met with some criticism. Many researchers believe that such profiles are simply too vague and general to be of any real value to investigators. Moreover, critics fear that a profile could hamper an investigation by leading police on a search for the wrong man. In response, proponents maintain that their efforts have never been designed to provide specific details about a particular killer. On the contrary, they warn that the profiling process is not an exact science and is not a substitute for a thorough and well-planned investigation.[27]

The specific value and effectiveness of these five police responses presently being used to combat serial murder will certainly be measured on a case-by-case basis. Collectively, however, they demonstrate that members of the law enforcement community are willing to work together in this endeavor. The cooperation and sharing of information that must take place in all five methods are encouraging signs for the future.

Perhaps the most important step in the fight against existing serial killers is the creation of the Violent Criminal Apprehension Program (VICAP), a computerized analysis system that compares murders from across the country to determine the existence of any similar patterns.[28] Readily accessible to all law enforcement agencies through the FBI, the analysis process begins with the submission of a detailed account of the murder. The information obtained is then entered into the system and compared with reports supplied by other police agencies. Any similarities found between cases are reported back to the local agencies for their review and follow-up investigation. The VICAP computer therefore acts as the hub of a nationwide information network by collecting, analyzing, and distributing vital data on serial murder to all parts of the country. In addition, the system provides many of the advantages that conferences and information clearinghouses do, yet it does so in a quicker, more efficient, and less arduous manner. The comparison of cases from California to New York can now be made almost on a daily basis, without waiting for the formation of a national conference. Moreover, it can perform in a matter of hours what it previously took several police officers days or even weeks to accomplish.

The result of the VICAP system is a sophisticated method for tracking and identifying serial murderers that far surpasses any other efforts by law enforcement authorities to date. By coordinating data from around the country, it effectively eradicates local police agencies' inability or unwillingness to share information. It also allows for an immediate analysis and identification of patterned violent crimes and thus marks a significant achievement by law enforcement agencies in the fight against existing serial killers.

Law officials, however, cannot stop present serial killers on their own. Their efforts are merely reactive in nature, since they must wait for a murder to occur before they can act. Thus, society as well must contribute its support by recognizing the peril that runaways and hitchhikers place themselves in when they travel the highways alone. These individuals are prime targets for any serial killer. To protect them, shelters and halfway houses should be established in every community. Prostitutes also run a great risk of becoming the victims of serial murder.[29] By making themselves available to anyone on the street, they expose themselves to grave consequences. Thus, the time has come for society to grapple with the issue of prostitution by either eradicating it or finding a way to coexist with it. In either case, the goal should be to remove prostitutes from the street corner and take them out of the hands of the serial killer.

Society also can take significant steps in the fight against existing serial murderers by allowing the FBI to investigate suspected serial murderers directly.[30] The vast amount of resources available to this agency should not be left untapped when society is facing such a dangerous criminal. Although this could create problems with individual state sovereignty, agreements could be drawn up between the federal and state governments for mutual cooperation in serial murder cases. Accordingly, our legislative bodies should ensure the FBI a greater role in the investigation and apprehension of serial murderers.

Once a serial murderer is captured and convicted, society is left with the difficult task of deciding what to do with him. Obviously, he must be incarcerated to protect the public as well as for punishment. The death penalty is imposed in some instances because of the enormity of the crime or because of the heinous nature in which the murders were committed. Until recently, these two methods were the only alternatives available, but researchers are beginning to discover that there may be other ways to deal with the repetitive, violent criminal.

In this regard, one of the first alternatives being explored is mandatory psychotherapy for violent offenders. In studies conducted using persons with antisocial personality disorders, researchers found that some form of ego-building approach to treatment is the most beneficial.[31] This treatment alternative closely resembles both family therapy and the sessions conducted for grown-up abused children previously discussed. However, this approach is questioned by a number of professionals who contend that psychotherapeutic measures are of little value. They maintain that, if an offender shows improvement at all, it is more likely due to his higher IQ and the passage of time in prison than any aspect of the psychotherapy.[32] Moreover, many believe that the psychopath is simply unresponsive to psychotherapy of any kind, a belief fostered by the long-standing observation that the psychopath simply will not abide by society's expectations, even when threatened with social censure, punishment, embarrassment, or imprisonment. Recent findings, however, suggest that the psychopath can benefit from some forms of psychotherapy despite his traditional behavior. In addition, many researchers believe that psychotherapy can be productive when it is used in combination with drug therapy, arguing that the use of drugs makes the offender more amenable to psychotherapy and facilitates the learning process.[33]

Although the use of psychotherapy for the treatment of violent offenders has not won universal acceptance, the benefits that may be derived by employing such techniques should not be overlooked when society is deciding the fate of the serial murderer. Since we have seen that psychotherapeutic measures may assist this type of criminal before he strikes, it is to our advantage to try such an approach after conviction. Moreover, since the serial killer is, in several respects, different from the psychopath, the discouragement of some researchers in dealing with the psychopath should not deter such efforts with serial murderers. Indeed, society can only benefit from such attempts.

Another approach to the treatment of violent criminals, alluded to above, is the use of drugs to control behavior. Although evidence on the effects of drugs on aggression is rather sparse, there have been some promising results with certain drugs which offer a direction for future research.[34] In a number of studies, individuals with violent, antisocial personality disorders who were given lithium on a regular basis soon reported lower levels of anger and a greater ability to control angry feelings, even when provoked. Although this offers some hope for the treatment of violent offenders, researchers point out that drugs may affect different people in various ways. Indeed, they are quick to caution that it is almost impossible to predict accurately just how any one person will react.[35] Thus, there is little guidance for the successful administration of drugs to control an individual's violent behavior.

Researchers also have found that some tranquilizers, such as chlordiazepoxide, diazepam, and oxazepam, are useful in reducing violent behavior, but there is no conclusive evidence that any are effective in individuals suffering from antisocial personality disorders. Conversely, several studies suggest that a stimulant regimen is more appropriate when treating personality disorders in adults who experienced minimal brain damage as children.[36] This observation closely parallels the paradoxical effect of stimulants in hyperactive children discussed in Chapter 6, but, once again, these studies do not offer conclusive findings.

Interesting, however, is a study dealing with intermittent explosive disorder, in which one researcher found that metoprolol, a selective B-1 adrenoreceptor, was useful in controlling violent outbursts. But the investigation was conducted using only two subjects, whose life histories suggested various causal factors for their violent behavior, including meningitis and temporal lobe epilepsy. The researcher himself conceded that controlled studies must be conducted before the efficacy of metoprolol can be determined.[37] Nevertheless, these preliminary results offer hope for future research in the use of drugs to control violent outbursts.

When treating the serial murderer with various drugs, one must be extremely cautious. Since such medication can have wide-ranging effects on different people, a drug that might decrease aggression in one individual may very well increase it in another.[38] Accordingly, controlled tests need to be conducted to document the effects of any drug on the behavioral patterns of the serial killer before this method can be used. To do otherwise may expose the public to an even greater danger.

Society, then, has several options available to it when addressing the problem of the serial murderer. Although some believe that the only response to dealing with this type of criminal is by incarceration or death,[39] the measures discussed above indicate that the solution to serial murder is not beyond our grasp. Therefore, society should welcome these various efforts and continue to encourage further study of the serial killer.

Notes

1. Oates (1982) at 2–3; Cohn at 445.
2. Erickson et al. at 81–83.
3. Kempe at 362.
4. Id. at 363–64; Oates (1986) at 93; Giarretto at 144.
5. Kempe at 375–76.
6. Oates (1986) at 94; Kempe at 367.
7. Van Meter at 79; Garbarino et al. at 119.
8. Cohn at 446; Fritz at 122; Siegel and Senna at 260.
9. Garbarino et al. at 130–39; Golub et al. at 257–59; Wilson (Ann) at 434.
10. Kempe at 378–79; Jones and Alexander at 356 (citing to C. Henry Kempe and Ruth Kempe, "The Untreatable Family," in *Child Abuse* [London: Fontana Open Books, 1978], 103–6).
11. Oates (1986) at 95; Kempe at 94–95 (citing to F. G. Bolton, Roy H. Laner, and Dorothy S. Gai, "For Better or Worse? Foster Parents and Foster Children in an Officially Reported Child Maltreatment Population," *Children and Youth Services Review* 3 [1981]: 37–53).
12. Siegel and Senna at 260; Garbarino et al. at 121.
13. Cohn at 445, 450–52, 446–47; *President's Child Safety Partnership—Final Report* (1987); Garbarino et al. at 174.
14. Leehan and Wilson at 27, 91.
15. Id. at 57–73; Jones and Alexander at 353.
16. Egger at 5, 74, 154; House of Rep. Hearing at 2.
17. Egger at 46, 151, 199; House of Rep. Hearing at 57; Danto et al. at 7; Cartel at 83.
18. Egger at 156, 81–82; Winn and Merrill at 56.

19. Cartel at 38; Egger at 236.

20. House of Rep. Hearing at 2, 59, 64; Egger at 156.

21. Egger at iv, 50, 54.

22. House of Rep. Hearing at 92–93, 75.

23. Egger at 55 (citing to Daniel C. Myre, *Death Investigation* [Washington, DC: International Association of Chiefs of Police, 1974]).

24. Id. at 57–59 (citing to Pierce R. Brooks, *The Investigative Consultant Team: A New Approach for Law Enforcement Cooperation* [Washington, DC: Police Executive Research Forum, 1982]).

25. Id. at 59.

26. Holmes and DeBurger (1988) at 87; Egger at 59–62; Douglas and Burgess at 9.

27. For researchers see Levin and Fox at 174, Porter at 2–3, Egger at 63–64, and Holmes and DeBurger (1988) at 85; for critics see Porter at 3 and Liebert at 198–99; and for proponents see Ault and Resse at 2, Porter at 6, and House of Rep. Hearing at 29.

28. Howlett et al. at 15.

29. MacDonald at 279; House of Rep. Hearing at 61.

30. House of Rep. Hearing at 8, 62–63.

31. Rada at 192–93; Wilson and Herrnstein at 378–79; Moyer at 155. See also Rada at 192 (citing to Margaret Draughon, "Ego-building: An Aspect of the Treatment of Psychopaths," *Psychological Reports* 40 [April 1977]: 615–26); and Bartol at 384.

32. Wilson and Herrnstein at 378–79; Jesse at 41.

33. Bartol at 381–82; Cleckley at 438–39; Goleman (1987) at C2; Moyer at 155.

34. Kellner at 25; Tupin at 168; Reid at 158.

35. Kellner at 26.

36. Id. at 21–22, 25.

37. Mattes at 1108–9.

38. Moyer at 148.

39. Wilson (Paul) at 58.

Epilogue

The destruction of life by the serial murderer is certainly one of the most tragic events of our time. Although the
taking of a life is never without anguish, when it occurs repeatedly in such a senseless manner, the pain and tragedy of society's
loss increases exponentially. Our deepest sorrows are then
compounded when we realize that the victims of this horror are
often our children and young adults. But there are other victims
of serial murder as well; these are the parents, families, and
friends of those who are killed. For these survivors, the motivation
for serial murder is unimportant. As the French writer and
philosopher, Blaise Pascal, so aptly noted, the secret "intention of
the one who wounds does not relieve the pain of the one who is
wounded."[1] Moreover, the sorrow and emptiness that become a
part of their lives are often emotions that must be dealt with alone
since they are largely forgotten by society.[2]

This attitude of society toward these forgotten victims, however, is beginning to change. Organizations such as Victims for
Victims, Mothers of Murdered Children, Parents of Murdered
Children, and the Compassionate Friends are attempting the
arduous task of helping the survivors of murder find comfort.[3] In
addition, national conferences designed to assist these victims
have been formulated. Although these efforts provide only small
consolation for the grief felt by these individuals, at least society
is beginning to recognize its responsibility to these other victims
of serial murder.

Finally, when dealing with the serial murderer, it seems that
society has two alternatives. One is simply to accept the fact that
there exist among us a number of "moral monsters" whom we
must seek out and destroy.[4] This alternative, however, is short-
sighted and exhibits unthinking emotion. It brings us no closer to

discovering what is behind serial murder or how to prevent it from occurring. The second alternative is for society to probe deeply into what originally motivates this type of crime. Only in this way will we be able both to stop present serial murderers and, more importantly, prevent their future development. It is hoped that this book will become the starting point of such research, and that further exploration into the motivation and development of serial murder will soon follow.

Whatever society chooses to do in response to serial murder, it must act quickly. We have seen the destruction and terror that the serial killer leaves in his wake. It is as well frighteningly apparent that, if he is not stopped as soon as possible, every citizen is in peril. For once his killing spree begins, the serial murderer lives for nothing but—to kill again.

Notes

1. Jesse at 42 (citing to the work of the seventeenth-century French author Blaise Pascal).
2. House of Rep. Hearing at 72.
3. Danto et al. 95–96; Cartel at 271; Holmes and DeBurger (1988) at 146.
4. Jesse at 212.

Bibliography

Abrahamsen, David. *Confessions of Son of Sam*. New York: Columbia University Press, 1985.
———. *The Murdering Mind*. New York: Harper and Row, 1973.
Attorney General's Commission on Pornography, Final Report. Prepared by the Department of Justice. Washington, DC, July 1986.
Ault, Richard L., Jr., and Reese, James T. "A Psychological Assessment of Crime Profiling." *Federal Bureau of Investigation Law Enforcement Bulletin* 49 (March 1980): 22–25.
Axthelm, Pete, and Ryan, Michael. "A Condemned Man's Last Bequest." *People Weekly* 31 (February 6, 1989): 44.
Bach-y-Rita, George; Lion, John R.; Climent, Carlos E.; and Ervin, Frank R. "Episodic Dyscontrol: A Study of 130 Violent Patients." *American Journal of Psychiatry* 127 (May 1971): 49–54.
Bartol, Curtis R. *Criminal Behavior: A Psychosocial Approach*. Englewood Cliffs, NJ: Prentice-Hall, 1980.
Bockman, Richard, and Taylor, Andy. "Stano — A Troubled and Terrifying Murderer." *Tampa Tribune-Times*, October 10, 1982.
Bright, Bill. "Bundy Tied to Murders of Two Coeds at the Shore." *Star Ledger* (Newark, NJ), January 26, 1989.
"Bundy Executed." *Star Ledger* (Newark, NJ), January 25, 1989.
"Bundy Toll May be 50, Prosecutor in Case Says." *New York Times*, January 26, 1989.
Burgess, Ann W.; Hartman, Carol R.; Ressler, Robert K.; Douglas, John E.; and McCormack, Arlene. "Sexual Homicide: A Motivational Model." *Journal of Interpersonal Violence* 1 (September 1986): 251–71.
Cahill, Tim. *Buried Dreams: Inside the Mind of a Serial Killer*. New York: Bantam Books, 1986.
Campion, John; Cravens, James M.; Rotholc, Alec; Weinstein, Henry C.; Covan, Fred; and Alpert, Murray. "A Study of 15 Matricidal Men." *American Journal of Psychiatry* 142 (March 1985): 312–17.
Cartel, Michael. *Disguise of Sanity: Serial Mass Murderers*. Toluca Lake, CA: Pepperbox Books, 1985.
Cheney, Margaret. *The Co-Ed Killer*. New York: Walker and Company, 1976.

Cleckley, Hervey. *The Mask of Sanity*. St. Louis, MO: C. V. Mosby, 1976.

Cohn, Anne H. "Our National Priorities for Prevention." In *The Battered Child*, edited by Ruth S. Kempe and Ray E. Helfer, 444–55. 4th ed. Chicago: University of Chicago Press, 1987.

Craft, Michael. "Who Are Mentally Abnormal Offenders?" In *Mentally Abnormal Offenders*, edited by Michael Craft and Ann Craft, 16–27. London: Bailliere Tidal, 1984.

Danto, Bruce L.; Bruhns, J.; and Kutcher, Austin K., eds. *The Human Side of Homicide*. New York: Columbia University Press, 1982.

" 'Deliberate Stranger' Killer Helping Lawmen Close Books on 30 Murders." *Star Ledger* (Newark, NJ), January 22, 1989.

" 'A Diabolical Genius': Slayer's Dark Side Eclipsed Promise of a Bright Future." *Star Ledger* (Newark, NJ), January 25, 1989.

Diagnostic and Statistical Manual of Mental Disorders. 3d ed. Washington, DC: American Psychiatric Association, 1980.

Diagnostic and Statistical Manual of Mental Disorders. 3d rev. ed. Washington, DC: American Psychiatric Association, 1987.

Donnerstein, Edward; Linz, Daniel; and Penrod, Steve. *The Question of Pornography: Research Findings and Policy Implications*. New York: Free Press, 1987.

Dorfman, Andrea. "The Criminal Mind, Body Chemistry and Nutrition May Lie at the Roots of Crime." *Science Digest* 92 (October 1984): 44.

Dorland's Illustrated Medical Dictionary. 26th ed. Philadelphia: W. B. Saunders, 1985.

Douglas, John E., and Burgess, Alan E. "Criminal Profiling: A Viable Investigative Tool against Violent Crime." *Federal Bureau of Investigation Law Enforcement Bulletin* 55 (December 1986): 9–13.

Egger, Steven A. *An Analysis of the Serial Murder Phenomenon and the Law Enforcement Response*. Ann Arbor, MI: University Microfilms International, 1986.

Elliot, Frank A. *Clinical Neurology*. 2d ed. Philadelphia: W. B. Saunders, 1971.

Encyclopedia of Crime and Justice. Vol. 4, *Psychopathy to Youth Gangs*, edited by Sanford H. Kadish et al., 1315–18, 1351–55. New York: Free Press, 1983.

Erickson, Edsel L.; McEvoy, Alan; and Colucci, Nicholas D., Jr. *Child Abuse and Neglect: A Guidebook for Educators and Community Leaders*. 2d ed. Holmes Beach, FL: Learning Publications, 1984.

Federal Bureau of Investigation Law Enforcement Bulletin 54. Prepared by the Department of Justice. Washington, DC, August 1985.

Finkelhor, David. "The Trauma of Child Sexual Abuse." *Journal of Interpersonal Violence* 2 (December 1987): 348–66.

Fisher, Kathleen. "Strangler's Mind Becomes a Trap for Psychologists." *Monitor Magazine* (April 1984): 10.

Foreman, Judy. "Authorities Say Serial Killers Are 'Bad'—but not 'Mad.' " *Tampa Tribune,* November 15, 1984.

Frank, Gerold. *The Boston Strangler.* New York: New American Library, 1966.

Fritz, Margot. "Parents Anonymous: Helping Clients to Accept Professional Services: A Personal Opinion." *Child Abuse and Neglect: The International Journal* 10 (January 1986): 121–23.

Garbarino, James; Guttman, Edna; and Seeley, Janis Wilson. *The Psychologically Battered Child Strategies for Identification, Assessment, and Intervention.* San Francisco: Jossey-Bass, 1986.

Giarretto, Henry. "A Comprehensive Child Sexual Abuse Treatment Programme." In *Child Abuse: A Community Concern,* edited by R. Kim Oates, 130–53. New York: Brunner/Mazel, 1982.

Gibbs, Frederic A., and Gibbs, Erna L. *Atlas of Electroencephalography. Neurological and Psychiatric Disorders.* Vol. 3. Reading, MA: Addison-Wesley, 1964.

Ginsberg, George L. "Adjustment and Impulse Control Disorders." In *Comprehensive Textbook of Psychiatry IV,* edited by Harold I. Kaplan and Benjamin J. Sadock, 1099–1100. Vol 2. Baltimore: Williams and Wilkins, 1985.

Goleman, Daniel. "Brain Defect Tied to Utter Amorality of the Psychopath." *New York Times,* July 7, 1987.

———. "Clues to Suicide: A Brain Chemical Is Implicated." *New York Times,* October 8, 1985.

Golub, Judith S.; Espinosa, Michael; Damon, Linda; and Carol, Jessica. "A Videotape Parent Education Program for Abusive Parents." *Child Abuse and Neglect: The International Journal* 11 (June 1987): 255–65.

Guttmacher, Manfred. *The Mind of the Murderer.* New York: Farrar, Straus and Cudahy, 1960.

Hare, Robert D. *Psychopathy: Theory and Research.* New York: John Wiley and Sons, 1970.

Hazelwood, Robert D., and Douglas, John E. "The Lust Murderer." *Federal Bureau of Investigation Law Enforcement Bulletin* 49 (April 1980): 18–22.

Holmes, Ronald M., and DeBurger, James E. "Profiles in Terror: The Serial Murderer." *Federal Probation* 49 (September 1985): 29–34.

———. *Serial Murder.* Newbury Park, CA: Sage Publications, 1988.

House of Representatives Hearing of the Subcommittee of the Committee on Government Operations. "The Federal Role in Investigation of Serial Violent Crime." 99th Cong., 2d sess., April 9 and May 21, 1986.

Howlett, James B.; Hanfland, Kenneth A.; and Ressler, Robert K. "The Violent Criminal Apprehension Program — VICAP: A Progress Report." *Federal Bureau of Investigation Law Enforcement Bulletin* 55 (December 1986): 14–22.

Jenkins, Philip. "Serial Murder in England, 1940–1985." *Journal of Criminal Justice* 16 (1988): 1–15.

Jesse, F. Tennyson. *Murder and Its Motives*. New York: Doubleday, 1965.

Jones, David P. H., and Alexander, Helen. "Treating the Abusive Family within the Family Care System." In *The Battered Child*, edited by Ruth S. Kempe and Ray E. Helfer, 339–59. 4th ed. Chicago: University of Chicago Press, 1987.

Karpman, Benjamin. "On the Need of Separating Psychopathy into Two Distinct Clinical Types: The Symptomatic and the Idiopathic." *Journal of Criminal Psychopathology* 3 (July 1941): 112–37.

Kellner, Robert. "Drug Treatment in Personality Disorders." In *The Treatment of Antisocial Syndromes*, edited by William H. Reid, 20–29. New York: Van Nostrand Reinhold, 1981.

Kempe, Ruth S. "A Developmental Approach to the Treatment of the Abused Child." In *The Battered Child*, edited by Ruth S. Kempe and Ray E. Helfer, 360–81. 4th ed. Chicago: University of Chicago Press, 1987.

Kendall, Elizabeth. *The Phantom Prince: My Life with Ted Bundy*. Seattle: Madrona, 1981.

Keyes, Edward. *The Michigan Murders*. New York: Reader's Digest Press, 1976.

Kidder, Tracy. *The Road to Yuba City*. New York: Doubleday, 1974.

Kiloh, L. G.; McComas, A. J.; and Osselton, J. W. *Clinical Electroencephalography*. 3d ed. London: Butterworth, 1972.

Lacayo, Richard. "Master of Cant and Recant." *Time* 129 (January 12, 1987): 66.

Lamar, Jacob V., Jr. "Trail of Death." *Time* 123 (April 16, 1984): 26.

Larsen, Richard W. *Bundy: The Deliberate Stranger*. Englewood Cliffs, NJ: Prentice-Hall, 1980.

Leehan, James, and Wilson, Laura Pistone. *Grown Up Abused Children*. Chicago: Charles C. Thomas, 1985.

Lester, David. *The Murderer and His Murder*. New York: AMS Press, 1986.

Levin, Jack, and Fox, James Alan. *Mass Murder: America's Growing Menace*. New York: Plenum Press, 1985.

Leyton, Elliot. *Compulsive Killers: The Story of Modern Multiple Murder*. New York: Washington Mews Books, 1986.

Liebert, John A. "Contributions of Psychiatric Consultation in the Investigation of Serial Murder." *International Journal of Offender Therapy and Comparative Criminology* 29 (January 1985): 187–99.

Linedecker, Clifford L. *The Man Who Killed Boys*. New York: St. Martin's Press, 1980.

Lunde, Donald T. *Murder and Madness*. San Francisco: San Francisco Book Company, 1976.

MacDonald, John M. *The Murderer and His Victim.* 2d ed. Chicago: Charles C. Thomas, 1986.

MacLean, Paul D. "New Findings Relevant to the Evolution of Psychosexual Functions of the Brain." *Journal of Nervous and Mental Disease* 135 (October 1962): 289–301.

Mattes, Jeffrey A. "Metoprolol for Intermittent Explosive Disorder." *American Journal of Psychiatry* 142 (September 1985): 1108–9.

Mawson, A., and Jacobs, K. "Corn Consumption, Tryptophan and Cross-national Homicide Rates." *Journal of Orthomolecular Psychiatry* 7 (January 1978): 227–30.

McGrath, Peter, with Smith, Vern E. "Atlanta: Profile of a Suspect." *Newsweek* 98 (July 6, 1981): 22.

Menninger, Karl, and Mayman, Martin. "Episodic Dyscontrol: A Third Order of Stress Adaptation." *Bulletin of the Menninger Clinic* 20 (July 1956): 153–65.

Michaud, Stephen G. "The FBI's New Psyche Squad." *New York Times*, October 26, 1986 (magazine section).

Michaud, Stephen G., and Aynesworth, Hugh. *The Only Living Witness.* New York: Simon and Schuster, 1983.

"The Mind of the Mass Murderer." *Time* 102 (August 27, 1973): 56–57.

Minnery, Tom, ed. *Pornography: A Human Tragedy.* Wheaton, IL: Tyndale House, 1986.

Monopolis, Spyros, and Lion, John R. "Problems in the Diagnosis of Intermittent Explosive Disorder." *American Journal of Psychiatry* 140(9) (September 1983): 1200–1202.

Monroe, Russel A. "The Problem of Impulsivity in Personality Disturbances." In *Personality Disorders: Diagnosis and Management (Revised for DSM-III)*, edited by John R. Lion, 371–92. 2d ed. Baltimore: Williams and Wilkins, 1981.

Morrison, James R., and Minkoff, Kenneth. "Explosive Personality as a Sequel to the Hyperactive-Child Syndrome." *Comprehensive Psychiatry* 16 (July-August 1975): 343–48.

Moyer, Kenneth E. *Violence and Aggression: A Physiological Perspective.* New York: Paragon House, 1987.

Murder: No Apparent Motive (film). Produced by Imre Horvath. Rights held by Rainbow Broadcasting, New York, 1984.

"Murderous Personality: Was the Hillside Strangler a Jekyll and Hyde?" *Time* 113 (May 7, 1979): 26.

Nobile, Philip, and Nader, Eric. *United States of America vs. Sex: How the Meese Commission Lied about Pornography.* New York: Minotaur Press, 1986.

Nordheimer, Jon. "Bundy Is Put to Death in Florida after Admitting Trail of Killings." *New York Times*, January 25, 1989.

Norris, Joel, and Birnes, William J. *Serial Killers: The Growing Menace.* New York: Bantam Books, 1988.

Oates, R. Kim. "Child Abuse—A Community Concern." In *Child Abuse: A Community Concern*, edited by R. Kim Oates, 1–12. New York: Brunner/Mazel, 1982.

———. *Child Abuse and Neglect: What Happens Eventually?* New York: Brunner/Mazel, 1986.

O'Brien, Darcy. *Two of a Kind: The Hillside Stranglers*. New York: New American Library, 1985.

Olsen, Jack. *The Man with the Candy*. New York: Simon and Schuster, 1974.

Otnow Lewis, Dorothy; Pincus, Jonathan H.; Feldman, Marilyn; Jackson, Lori; and Bard, Barbara. "Psychiatric, Neurological, and Psychoeducational Characteristics of 15 Death Row Inmates in the United States." *American Journal of Psychiatry* 143 (July 1986): 838–45.

Otnow Lewis, Dorothy; Shanok, Shelly S.; and Balla, David A. "Perinatal Difficulties, Head and Face Trauma, and Child Abuse in the Medical Histories of Serious Delinquent Children." *American Journal of Psychiatry* 136 (April 1979): 419–23.

Pasternack, Stefan A. "The Explosive, Antisocial and Passive-Aggressive Personalities." In *Personality Disorders: Diagnosis and Management (Revised for DSM-III)*, edited by John R. Lion, 45–69. Baltimore: Williams and Wilkins, 1974.

Peer, Elizabeth, with Shapiro, Dan. "A Mass Killer Cops a Plea." *Newsweek* 100 (August 23, 1982): 29.

Porter, Bruce. "Mind Hunters: Tracking Down Killers with the FBI's Psychological Profiling Team." *Psychology Today* 17 (April 1983): 44–52.

President's Child Safety Partnership—Final Report. William W. McConnell, chairman. Washington, DC: Government Printing Office, 1987.

Quay, Herbert C. "Psychopathic Personality as Pathological Stimulation-seeking." *American Journal of Psychiatry* 122 (August 1965): 180–83.

Rada, Richard T. "Sociopathy and Alcoholism: Diagnostic and Treatment Implications." In *The Treatment of Antisocial Syndromes*, edited by William H. Reid, 184–203. New York: Van Nostrand Reinhold, 1981.

Reichard, Suzanne, and Tillman, Carl. "Murder and Suicide as Defenses against Schizophrenic Psychosis." *Journal of Clinical Psychopathology* 11 (October 1950): 149–63.

Reid, William H. "The Antisocial Personality and Related Syndromes." In *Personality Disorders: Diagnosis and Management (Revised for DSM-III)*, edited by John R. Lion, 133–62. 2d ed. Baltimore: Williams and Wilkins, 1981.

Ressler, Robert K.; Burgess, Ann W.; Douglas, John E.; Hartman, Carol R.; and D'Agostino, Ralph B. "Serial Killers and Their Victims." *Journal of Interpersonal Violence* 1 (September 1986a): 288–308.

Ressler, Robert K.; Burgess, Ann W.; Hartman, Carol R.; Douglas, John E.; and McCormack, Arlene. "Murderers Who Rape and Mutilate." *Journal of Interpersonal Violence* 1 (September 1986b): 273–87.

Restak, Richard. *The Brain.* New York: Bantam Books, 1984.

Revitch, Eugene, and Schlesinger, Louis E. *Psychopathology of Homicide.* Chicago: Charles C. Thomas, 1981.

Rogers, Carl M., and Terry, Tremaine. "Clinical Intervention with Boy Victims of Sexual Abuse." In *Victims of Sexual Aggression,* edited by Irving R. Stuart and Joanne G. Greer. New York: Van Nostrand Reinhold, 1984.

Rule, Ann. *The Stranger beside Me.* New York: W. W. Norton, 1980.

Satten, Joseph; Menninger, Karl; Rosen, Irwin; and Mayman, Martin. "Murder without Apparent Motive: A Study in Personality Disorganization." *American Journal of Psychiatry* 117 (July 1960): 48–53.

Schmeck, Harold M., Jr. "Brain Defects Seen in Those Who Repeat Violent Acts." *New York Times,* September 17, 1985.

Schreiber, Flora Rheta. *The Shoemaker: The Anatomy of a Psychotic.* New York: Simon and Schuster, 1983.

Schwartz, Ted. *The Hillside Strangler: A Murderer's Mind.* New York: Doubleday, 1981.

Senate Hearing of the Subcommittee on Juvenile Justice on Patterns of Murders Committed by One Person, in Large Numbers with No Apparent Rhyme, Reason or Motivation. U.S. Senate, Hearing No. 98-513, 98th Cong., 1st sess., July 12, 1983.

Shryock, Nancy. "Dr. Helen Morrison: Exploring the Minds of Mass Murderers." *Social Issues Resource Series* 2, Article 99 (1985): 1–4.

Siegel, Larry J., and Senna, Joseph J. *Juvenile Delinquency Theory, Practice and Law.* St. Paul, MN: West Publishing Company, 1981.

Simon, Roger. "Gacy: I'm Not a 'Raging Maniac.'" *Tampa Tribune-Times,* February 20, 1983.

Solomon, Eldra Pearl, and Davis, P. William. *Understanding Human Anatomy and Physiology.* New York: McGraw-Hill, 1978.

Stafford-Clark, D., and Taylor, F. H. "Clinical and Electroencephalographic Studies of Prisoners Charged with Murder." *Journal of Neurology, Neurosurgery and Psychiatry* 12 (November 1949): 325–30.

Stanley, Alessandra. "Catching a New Breed of Killers." *Time* 122 (November 14, 1983): 47.

Strasser, Steven; with Prout, Linda; Shannon, Elaine; and Shapiro, Daniel. "A Long Trail of Death." *Newsweek* 103 (April 16, 1984): 38.

Sullivan, Terry, with Maiken, Peter T. *Killer Clown.* New York: Grosset and Dunlap, 1983.

Taber's Cyclopedic Medical Dictionary. Edited by C. L. Thomas. 16th ed. Philadelphia: F. A. Davis, 1989.

Tupin, Joe P. "Treatment of Impulsive Aggression." In *The Treatment of Antisocial Syndromes*, edited by William H. Reid, 162–72. New York: Van Nostrand Reinhold, 1981.

Uniform Crime Reports: Crime in the United States, 1988. Prepared by the Federal Bureau of Investigation. Washington, DC: Department of Justice, 1989.

Van Meter, Mary Jane S. "An Alternative to Foster Care for Victims of Child Abuse/Neglect: A University-Based Program." *Child Abuse and Neglect: The International Journal* 10 (January 1986): 79–84.

Wertham, Frederic. "The Catathymic Crisis: A Clinical Entity." *Archives of Neurology and Psychiatry* 37 (April 1937): 974–78.

———. *Dark Legend: A Study in Murder*. New York: Duell, Sloan and Pearce, 1941.

———. *The Show of Violence*. New York: Doubleday, 1949.

———. *A Sign for Cain: An Exploration of Human Violence*. New York: MacMillan, 1966.

Williams, Denis. "Neural Factors Related to Habitual Aggression." *Brain* 92 (October 1969): 503–20.

Wilson, Ann L. "Promoting a Positive Parent-Infant Relationship." In *The Battered Child*, edited by Ruth S. Kempe and Ray E. Helfer, 434–43. 4th ed. Chicago: University of Chicago Press, 1987.

Wilson, Paul R. " 'Stranger' Child-Murder: Issues Relating to Causes and Controls." *International Journal of Offender Therapy and Comparative Criminology* 31 (May 1987): 49–59.

Wilson, Colin, and Seaman, Donald. *The Encyclopedia of Modern Murder, 1962–1982*. New York: Putnam Group, 1983.

Wilson, James Q., and Herrnstein, Richard J. *Crime and Human Nature*. New York: Simon and Schuster, 1985.

Winn, Steven, and Merrill, David. *Ted Bundy: The Killer Next Door*. New York: Bantam Books, 1979.

Wolfgang, Marvin E., and Weiner, Neil Alan, eds. *Criminal Violence*. Beverly Hills, CA: Sage Publications, 1982.

Index

DATE DUE

10/012/92 ILL			
FEB 09 '93			
MAR 17 '93			
APR 2 1 '93			
APR.30.1993			
NOV.08.1993			
MAR24.1994			
10/5/94 ILL			
MAR16.1995			
APR.03.1995			
APR.17.1995			
OCT 31 1995 NOV.22.1995			
APR.13.2000			
DEC 14 '05			
5-21-08 ILL			
GAYLORD			PRINTED IN U.S.A